DIAGNOSTIC AND MASTERY TESTS TO ACCOMPANY

Writing First

PRACTICE IN CONTEXT

AND

Writing in Context

PARAGRAPHS AND ESSAYS

DIAGNOSTIC AND MASTERY TESTS TO ACCOMPANY

Writing First

PRACTICE IN CONTEXT

Second Edition

AND

Writing in Context

PARAGRAPHS AND ESSAYS

Bedford/St. Martin's

Boston ■ New York

Manufactured in the United States of America.

7 6 5 4 3
f e d c b a

For information, write: Bedford/St. Martin's, 75 Arlington Street,
Boston, MA 02116   (617-399-4000)

ISBN: 0-312-39977-4

Preface

Diagnostic and Mastery Tests to Accompany WRITING FIRST: PRACTICE IN CONTEXT, Second Edition, and *WRITING IN CONTEXT: PARAGRAPHS AND ESSAYS* includes the following diagnostic and review materials:

- The Sentence Skills Diagnostic Test comprises fifty items and covers the grammar, punctuation, and mechanics topics in Units 4–7 of *Writing First* and *Writing in Context*. (This diagnostic test is also available online at the Exercise Central Web site, which can be reached via <http://www.bedfordstmartins.com/writingfirst>.)

- Forty review exercise sets test students' mastery of the material in Units 4–7 of *Writing First* and *Writing in Context*. For each chapter, two exercise sets are included. The first set is typically a set of twenty discrete items to be edited, while the second set is a connected-discourse editing exercise.

Answers to the diagnostic and mastery tests are provided in the Answers section at the end of the booklet. The diagnostic key includes cross-references to relevant chapters in *Writing First* and *Writing in Context* and to relevant exercises in the Exercise Central collection and the *Writing First* Writing Guide Software grammar tutorials.

Also available with *Writing First* are an exercise booklet, *Supplemental Exercises to Accompany* WRITING FIRST, Second Edition, and a 2,000-item electronic exercise bank at the Bedford/St. Martin's online exercise site, Exercise Central, which can be accessed via <http://www.bedfordstmartins.com/writingfirst>. If you would like more information about these exercise materials or about the complete supplements package for *Writing First* or *Writing in Context,* please contact your local Bedford/St. Martin's sales rep or email <facultyservices@bfwpub.com>.

Contents

Preface   v

Sentence Skills Diagnostic Test   1

Writing Effective Sentences

15-1	Writing Simple Sentences	9
15-2	Writing Simple Sentences	10
16-1	Writing Compound Sentences	12
16-2	Writing Compound Sentences	15
17-1	Writing Complex Sentences	17
17-2	Writing Complex Sentences	20
18-1	Achieving Sentence Variety	21
18-2	Achieving Sentence Variety	22
19-1	Using Parallelism	23
19-2	Using Parallelism	25
20-1	Using Words Effectively	26
20-2	Using Words Effectively	28

Solving Common Sentence Problems

21-1	Run-Ons and Comma Splices	30
21-2	Run-Ons and Comma Splices	32
22-1	Sentence Fragments	34
22-2	Sentence Fragments	35
23-1	Subject-Verb Agreement	36
23-2	Subject-Verb Agreement	38
24-1	Illogical Shifts	39
24-2	Illogical Shifts	41

25-1   Dangling and Misplaced Modifiers   42

25-2   Dangling and Misplaced Modifiers   44

Understanding Basic Grammar

26-1   Verbs: Past Tense   45

26-2   Verbs: Past Tense   46

27-1   Verbs: Past Participles   48

27-2   Verbs: Past Participles   50

28-1   Nouns and Pronouns   51

28-2   Nouns and Pronouns   53

29-1   Adjectives and Adverbs   55

29-2   Adjectives and Adverbs   57

Understanding Punctuation, Mechanics, and Spelling

31-1   Using Commas   58

31-2   Using Commas   60

32-1   Using Apostrophes   61

32-2   Using Apostrophes   63

33-1   Understanding Mechanics   65

33-2   Understanding Mechanics   67

34-1   Understanding Spelling   68

34-2   Understanding Spelling   70

Answers   71

Sentence Skills Diagnostic Test

Many of the following numbered items are not complete sentences or contain grammatical errors or other writing problems. From the choices following each item, select the best sentence and circle the corresponding letter. If you think the original item is the best option, select "No change."

1. Ronald Reagan's first job after college.
   a. Ronald Reagan started his career as a sportscaster in Iowa.
   b. First job after college as a sportscaster in Iowa.
   c. NO CHANGE

2. One of my problems happen to be finding competent child care.
   a. One of my problems happens to be finding competent child care.
   b. One of my problems happen to be finding competent babysitting.
   c. NO CHANGE

3. They all listened carefully as the police officer speaks.
   a. They all listened carefully as the police officer spoke.
   b. They all listen carefully as the police officer spoke.
   c. NO CHANGE

4. I baked the cake following the new recipe.
   a. Following the new recipe, I baked the cake.
   b. I baked, following the new recipe, the cake.
   c. NO CHANGE

5. Finally, she said I can leave.
   a. Finally, she said I canned leave.
   b. Finally, she said I could leave.
   c. NO CHANGE

6. My brother and I enjoy chess, even though he is a better player than I.
   a. My brother and I enjoy chess, even though he is a better player than me.
   b. My brother and me enjoy chess, even though he is a better player than I.
   c. NO CHANGE

7. Choosing the appropriatest outfit for a job interview can be difficult.
   a. Choosing the most appropriate outfit for a job interview can be difficult.
   b. Choosing the most appropriatest outfit for a job interview can be difficult.
   c. NO CHANGE

8. Jill keeps her diving equipments in the hall closet.
   a. Jill keeps her diving equipment in the hall closet.
   b. Jill keeps her divings equipments in the hall closet.
   c. NO CHANGE

1

9. Sean Connery, the movies' original James Bond was born in Edinburgh on August 25, 1930.
   a. Sean Connery, the movies' original James Bond, was born in Edinburgh on August 25, 1930.
   b. Sean Connery the movies' original James Bond, was born in Edinburgh on August 25, 1930.
   c. NO CHANGE

10. It is'nt a good idea to leave your car unlocked in this neighborhood.
    a. It isn't a good idea to leave your car unlocked in this neighborhood.
    b. It isnt a good idea to leave your car unlocked in this neighborhood.
    c. NO CHANGE

11. To be happy is more important than making a lot of money.
    a. It is more important to be happy than making a lot of money.
    b. Being happy is more important than making a lot of money.
    c. NO CHANGE

12. The story of alligators living in the New York City sewer system has been around for decades, it is not true.
    a. The story of alligators living in the New York City sewer system has been around for decades, but it is not true.
    b. The story of alligators living in the New York City sewer system has been around for decades, however, it is not true.
    c. NO CHANGE

13. Is a problem for me to get my homework done.
    a. Is a problem for me to do my homework.
    b. It is a problem for me to get my homework done.
    c. NO CHANGE

14. A driver with a learner's permit must always have a licensed driver in the car.
    a. Drivers with a learner's permit must always have a licensed driver in your car.
    b. A driver with a learner's permit must always have a licensed driver in their car.
    c. NO CHANGE

15. There is many problems facing returning college students today.
    a. There are many problems facing returning college students today.
    b. There are one problem facing returning college students today.
    c. NO CHANGE

16. A bodybuilder in his youth, Sean Connery had his first taste of success when he represented Scotland in the 1950 Mr. Universe contest.
    a. A bodybuilder in his youth Sean Connery had his first taste of success when he represented Scotland in the 1950 Mr. Universe contest.
    b. A bodybuilder in his youth Sean Connery, had his first taste of success when he represented Scotland in the 1950 Mr. Universe contest.
    c. NO CHANGE

17. New York city is the setting of the television series *NYPD Blue*.
    a. New York City is the setting of the television series "NYPD Blue."
    b. New York City is the setting of the television series *NYPD Blue*.
    c. NO CHANGE

18. Writer Alexandre Dumas wrote his novels on blue paper, his poetry on yellow paper, while writing for magazines on white paper.
    a. Writer Alexandre Dumas used blue paper for his novels, his poems were written on yellow paper, and he composed magazine articles on white paper.
    b. Writer Alexandre Dumas used blue paper for his novels, yellow paper for his poems, and white paper for his magazine articles.
    c. NO CHANGE

19. The Empire State Building is a famous landmark at New York City.
    a. The Empire State Building is a famous landmark from New York City.
    b. The Empire State Building is a famous landmark in New York City.
    c. NO CHANGE

20. Joe claimed the party was his fathers' idea, but his sisters claimed it was theirs.
    a. Joe claimed the party was his father's idea, but his sisters claimed it was theirs.
    b. Joe claimed the party was his fathers idea, but his sisters claimed it was theirs.
    c. NO CHANGE

21. In the 1970s, a story went around about bubble gum containing spiders' eggs this is another example of a modern folktale.
    a. In the 1970s, a story went around about bubble gum containing spiders' eggs, this is another example of a modern folktale.
    b. In the 1970s, a story went around about bubble gum containing spiders' eggs; this is another example of a modern folktale.
    c. NO CHANGE

22. Acted in Hollywood beginning in the mid-1930s.
    a. As an actor in Hollywood in the mid-1930s.
    b. In the mid-1930s, he started acting in Hollywood.
    c. NO CHANGE

23. Students can get a permit to drive at sixteen, but you have to pass a written test first.
    a. Students can get a permit to drive at sixteen, but they have to pass a written test first.
    b. A student can get a permit to drive at sixteen, but they have to pass a written test first.
    c. NO CHANGE

24. I thought the meeting would never end.
    a. I think the meeting would never end.
    b. I thinked the meeting would never end.
    c. NO CHANGE

25. The new African American Student Association will have their first meeting tomorrow.
    a. The new African American Student Association will have its first meeting tomorrow.
    b. The new African American Student Association will have his or her first meeting tomorrow.
    c. NO CHANGE

26. In order to do good in an interview, a person must feel good about the way he or she looks.
    a. In order to do well in an interview, a person must feel good about the way he or she looks.
    b. In order to do well in an interview, a person must feel well about the way he or she looks.
    c. NO CHANGE

27. I had never rided the roller coaster.
    a. I had never rode the roller coaster.
    b. I had never ridden the roller coaster.
    c. NO CHANGE

28. My mother needs a new raincoat.
    a. My mother is needing a new raincoat.
    b. My mother does needs a new raincoat.
    c. NO CHANGE

29. I like reading the newspaper more than I like watching the television news.
    a. I prefer reading the newspaper rather than to watch television news.
    b. I like to read the newspaper more than watching television news.
    c. NO CHANGE

30. Students who have children can't always spend enough time on campus.
    a. Students who has children can't always spend enough time on campus.
    b. A student who have children can't always spend enough time on campus.
    c. NO CHANGE

31. The early movies that made Sean Connery famous included *Dr. No, From Russia with Love*, and *Goldfinger*.
    a. The early movies, that made Sean Connery famous, included *Dr. No, From Russia with Love*, and *Goldfinger*.
    b. The early movies that made Sean Connery famous, included *Dr. No, From Russia with Love*, and *Goldfinger*.
    c. NO CHANGE

32. "We are an intelligent species, wrote Carl Sagan, and the use of our intelligence quite properly gives us pleasure."
    a. "We are an intelligent species," wrote Carl Sagan, "And the use of our intelligence quite properly gives us pleasure."
    b. "We are an intelligent species," wrote Carl Sagan, "and the use of our intelligence quite properly gives us pleasure."
    c. NO CHANGE

33. I like to eat peanut-butter sandwiches for lunch; they are inexpensive yet very filling.
    a. I like to eat peanut-butter sandwiches for lunch they are inexpensive yet very filling.
    b. I like to eat peanut-butter sandwiches for lunch, they are inexpensive yet very filling.
    c. NO CHANGE

34. The officer asked if we had any questions.
    a. The officer asked "Did we have any questions?"
    b. The officer asked did we have any questions?
    c. NO CHANGE

35. A president who launched a conservative revolution.
    a. Remembered today as a president who launched a conservative revolution.
    b. Today, many remember him as a president who launched a conservative revolution.
    c. NO CHANGE

36. I gone to Busch Gardens theme park many times.
    a. I went to Busch Gardens theme park many times.
    b. I wented to Busch Gardens theme park many times.
    c. NO CHANGE

37. Neither of the girls wanted their picture taken, even though the photographer said both looked perfect.
    a. Neither of the girls wanted his or her picture taken, even though the photographer said both looked perfect.
    b. Neither of the girls wanted her picture taken, even though the photographer said both looked perfect.
    c. NO CHANGE

38. My hair is same color as my brother's.
    a. My hair is the same color as my brother's.
    b. My hair is a same color as my brother's.
    c. NO CHANGE

39. Sean Connery went on of course, to be one of the world's most popular versatile, and well-regarded movie actors.
    a. Sean Connery went on, of course, to be one of the world's most popular, versatile, and well-regarded movie actors.
    b. Sean Connery went on of course to be one of the world's most popular, versatile, and well-regarded movie actors.
    c. NO CHANGE

40. Everyone want to study hard and get good grades.
    a. Everyone wants to study hard and get good grades.
    b. All students wants to study hard and get good grades.
    c. NO CHANGE

41. Because of their stringy flesh, some people do not like mangoes.
    a. Some people, because of their stringy flesh, do not like mangoes.
    b. Some people do not like mangoes because of their stringy flesh.
    c. NO CHANGE

42. The park has drawn hundreds of thousands of visitors since its opening.
    a. The park has drawed hundreds of thousands of visitors since its opening.
    b. The park has drew hundreds of thousands of visitors since its opening.
    c. NO CHANGE

43. Where your parents they are going on vacation this summer?
    a. Where your parents are going on vacation this summer?
    b. Where are your parents going on vacation this summer?
    c. NO CHANGE

44. Was it Dee or Anisa who donated her time to make these two loaves of bread for the bake sale?
    a. Was it Dee or Anisa who donated their time to make these two loaves of bread for the bake sale?
    b. Was it Dee or Anisa who donated its time to make these two loaves of bread for the bake sale?
    c. NO CHANGE

45. In cold weather, I always wear a long black wool coat.
    a. In cold weather, I always wear a black long wool coat.
    b. In cold weather, I always wear a long wool black coat.
    c. NO CHANGE

46. The more comfortable a person's clothes, the more better an interview is likely to go.
    a. The more comfortabler a person's clothes, the better an interview is likely to go.
    b. The more comfortable a person's clothes, the better an interview is likely to go.
    c. NO CHANGE

47. My brother has his permit, but he has not taken the driving test yet.
    a. My brother has his permit, but the driving test has not been taken by him yet.
    b. A permit was received by my brother, but he has not taken the driving test yet.
    c. NO CHANGE

48. Both luck and hard work often leads to success.
    a. Either luck or hard work often lead to success.
    b. Both luck and hard work often lead to success.
    c. NO CHANGE

49. Covered with tomato sauce, he placed the saucepan in the sink.
    a. He placed the saucepan, covered with tomato sauce, in the sink.
    b. He placed the saucepan in the sink, covered with tomato sauce.
    c. NO CHANGE

50. The waiter gave a glass of water to every person at the table.
    a. The waiter gave a glass of water to all person at the table.
    b. The waiter gave a glass of water to every people at the table.
    c. NO CHANGE

◆ 15-1 Writing Simple Sentences

In each sentence that follows, underline the complete subject once and the complete verb twice. Enclose any prepositional phrases within parentheses. Then label the simple subject (S) and the verb (AV for action verb or LV for linking verb).

1. During halftime, the coach gave the players a pep talk.

2. Mushrooms and anchovies are my least favorite pizza toppings.

3. A huge branch from an oak tree crashed through the picture window during the storm.

4. By the next day, the little girl with the broken arm was feeling better.

5. The director of the movie took more than half an hour setting up the shot.

6. On Broadway, the Delaney sisters were portrayed in the play *Having Our Say*.

7. Thunder and lightning can frighten young children.

8. Some adults are allergic to cats and dogs.

9. For someone in my position, the most difficult part of the job is the hours.

10. With computer networks, people can have long conversations without ever speaking to each other.

11. From time to time, each of us needs a helping hand.

12. Jay Leno has been hosting the *Tonight* show for some years now.

13. Jay and David Letterman are rivals in the late-night spot.

14. A special celebration is being planned for his tenth anniversary.

15. Next week, a hot new club is opening downtown.

16. We have already received our invitations.

17. Have you and your brothers received your invitations yet?

18. Someone in town has been spreading rumors about the Cruises.

19. A tropical storm of great force is headed toward the Caribbean.

20. Forecasters predict a great deal of damage.

◆ 15-2 Writing Simple Sentences

In each sentence that follows, underline the complete subject once and the complete verb twice. Enclose any prepositional phrases within parentheses. Then label the simple subject (S) and the verb (AV for action verb or LV for linking verb).

1. The average cow spends eighteen hours a day chewing.

2. In Washington, D.C., any new building must be shorter than the Capitol.

3. The tombstone of the founder of Borden's Dairy was designed in the shape of a can of condensed milk.

4. Honeybees and turtles have no sense of hearing.

5. Former President Jimmy Carter once rolled his feet over soda bottles.

6. On average, a person in the United States can expect almost one hundred fifty colds in a lifetime.

7. In Arabic, the word *sheik* means "old man."

8. Every home team in the National League must provide the referee with twenty-four footballs for each game.

9. Ducks sometimes sleep while swimming.

10. Many more radios have been sold in the United States than televisions.

11. According to an ancient Hindu law, adulterers were punished by the removal of their noses.

12. A flamingo can only eat with its head upside down.

13. Almost half of the bones in one's body are in one's hands and feet.

14. Ping-pong balls have been clocked at more than one hundred miles an hour.

15. Portraits of living people are prohibited on U.S. postage stamps.

16. In 1944, Fidel Castro was voted Cuba's top student athlete.

17. The word *typewriter* can be typed on the top line of letters of a typewriter keyboard.

18. King Juan Carlos of Spain was killed accidentally by his brother with an air rifle.

19. Chinese folding money was first made of deerskin.

20. In 1980, Carolyn Farrell of Dubuque, Iowa, became the first nun mayor of an American city.

◆ 16-1 Writing Compound Sentences

Combine the two sentences in each pair by using one of the coordinating conjunctions listed. Choose a conjunction that is appropriate for the relationship between the ideas expressed in the two sentences. Be sure to punctuate the sentence correctly.

Coordinating conjunctions: and   but   for   nor   or   so   yet

1. Speech is silver. Silence is golden.

   _____

   _____

2. The house was dark. She decided not to ring the doorbell.

   _____

   _____

3. He signed a long-term contract. He did not want to lose the job.

   _____

   _____

4. They will not surrender. They will not agree to a cease-fire.

   _____

   _____

5. They might leave in the morning. They might wait until tomorrow afternoon.

   _____

   _____

6. She had lived in California for many years. She remembered her Kansas childhood clearly.

   _____

   _____

7. Melody dropped French. Then she added Spanish.

   _____

   _____

8. The star witness changed his testimony. The defendant was acquitted.

   _____

   _____

9. There are thirty applicants for the program. Only ten will be admitted.

_____

_____

10. Everything seemed different. Nothing had really changed at all.

_____

_____

Combine the two sentences in each pair by using a semicolon alone or with one of the conjunctive adverbs or transitional expressions listed. Choose a conjunctive adverb or transitional expression that is appropriate for the relationship between the ideas expressed in the two sentences. Be sure to punctuate the sentence correctly.

| *Conjunctive adverbs:* | besides | consequently | however | still |
| | instead | nevertheless | therefore | |

| *Transitional expressions:* | for example | in fact | |
| | in addition | as a result | |

11. The movie won many awards. It didn't make money at the box office.

_____

_____

12. The weather was cold and drizzly. The outdoor festival was not a success.

_____

_____

13. My father comes from a large family. He is the fifth of thirteen children.

_____

_____

14. Earth Sciences 101 has both day and evening sessions. Anthropology 101 is only offered at night.

_____

_____

15. The experimental drug has several side effects. It may cause nausea in some patients.

_____

_____

16. The new mall provides many opportunities for shopping. It offers a food court with seven different vendors.

_____

_____

17. The speed limit sign was illegible. The officer gave me a ticket for speeding.

_____

_____

18. I had never been through customs before. I didn't know what to expect.

_____

_____

19. People often complain about the quality of television programming. They continue to watch.

_____

_____

20. Most fast food is very high in fat and calories. One serving of french fries has more than ten grams of fat.

_____

_____

◆ 16-2 Writing Compound Sentences

The following passages consist of short, choppy sentences. Revise each passage by linking pairs of sentences with a coordinating conjunction, a semicolon, a conjunctive adverb, or a transitional expression. The revision should be a smoothly written passage that connects ideas clearly and logically. Be sure to punctuate correctly.

a.   (1) Children in the United States do not eat enough fruits and vegetables. (2) They average only about half the recommended daily serving. (3) Parents may want to get their children to eat fruits and vegetables. (4) They don't know how. (5) Following are a few basic steps for doing so.

(6) A family can begin with breakfast. (7) Cereal can be topped with bananas or berries. (8) Fruit juice can be served. (9) Vegetables are good for snack time. (10) Cut-up carrots can be served with a flavorful dip. (11) Sandwiches can also be a way of adding vegetables. (12) Tuna salad is good with celery, pepper slices, and bean sprouts. (13) A turkey sandwich can include cucumber, lettuce, and tomato.

(14) As a treat, fruit can be dipped in chocolate. (15) Children can enjoy it like candy. (16) They still get the added nutritional benefits of fresh fruit.

b.   (1) Everyone complains about the weather sometimes. (2) Most people actually live where the climate is fairly moderate. (3) Some locales on Earth offer truly extreme temperatures. (4) Some places are barely habitable by humans.

(5) One area difficult for human existence is the Arctic region. (6) Temperatures go as low as 70 degrees below zero and remain below freezing most of the year. (7) Such intense cold discourages human habitation. (8) Intense heat is just as discouraging. (9) Deserts can be impossibly hot. (10) The Sahara in Africa reaches ground temperatures of up to 150 degrees. (11) There may be no rain for years at a time. (12) The air becomes too dry for people to breathe safely.

(13) The driest place on Earth is the Atacama desert in Chile. (14) Cold atmospheric currents and high surrounding mountains form a barrier to rain clouds. (15) Very little rain falls. (16) In fact, no rain has ever been recorded in some areas of the Atacama.

◆ 17-1 Writing Complex Sentences

Combine the two sentences in each pair by using one of the subordinating conjunctions listed. Choose a conjunction that is appropriate for the relationship between the ideas expressed in the two sentences. Be sure to punctuate correctly.

Subordinating conjunctions: after   before   while   when
                                because   as   although   since
                                so that   until

1. The sun set. The sky changed to a deep, starry blue.

    _____

    _____

2. The band warmed up for half an hour. The concert began.

    _____

    _____

3. The car crashed into the wall. Passersby watched helplessly.

    _____

    _____

4. I support the president. I don't always agree with his decisions.

    _____

    _____

5. It was almost midnight. My son finally walked through the door.

    _____

    _____

6. I decided to spend the night. It was too late to drive home.

    _____

    _____

7. All the votes were finally counted. Our candidate won.

    _____

    _____

8. My grandmother worked as a nurse for thirty years. She retired and started a restaurant.

    _____

    _____

9. Melanie started working for the company six months ago. She has already been promoted twice.

_____

_____

10. The class was moved to a larger room. Everyone would have a seat.

_____

_____

Combine the two sentences in each pair by using one of the relative pronouns listed. Choose a pronoun that is appropriate for the relationship between the ideas expressed in the two sentences. Be sure to punctuate the sentence correctly, paying particular attention to restrictive and nonrestrictive ideas.

Relative pronouns: who   which   that   whose

11. Martin Luther King Jr. wrote the book _Why We Can't Wait._ It expresses his views on civil rights.

_____

_____

12. Edward Teach was also known as Blackbeard the Pirate. He was infamous for his cruelty.

_____

_____

13. Black Hawk was chief of the Sauk and Fox Indians. He refused to move west of the Mississippi.

_____

_____

14. The International Workers of the World was an early labor organization. It recruited both skilled and unskilled labor.

_____

_____

15. _Citizen Kane_ is a classic movie. In it Orson Welles plays an egomaniacal newspaper publisher.

_____

_____

16. Prozac is a prescription drug. It is used in treating depression.

_____

_____

17. Stephen King is one of America's most popular writers. His books are often made into successful movies.

_____

_____

18. The actor Paul Robeson played many important black roles. He was the victim of much discrimination in the United States.

_____

_____

19. Ida Lupino starred in dozens of movies in the 1940s and 1950s. She was proudest of her career as a director.

_____

_____

20. The Sundance Institute was founded by Robert Redford. It supports the work of young, independent film directors.

_____

_____

◆ 17-2 Writing Complex Sentences

The following passage consists of short, choppy sentences. Revise it by linking pairs of sentences with a subordinating conjunction or a relative pronoun. The revision should be a smoothly written passage that connects ideas clearly and logically. Be sure to punctuate correctly.

(1) The sense of taste is known to everyone. (2) Exactly how we taste is not so well understood. (3) Taste is detected by tiny, barrel-shaped taste buds. (4) Most of these are located on the upper surface of the tongue. (5) A few are further down in the throat. (6) The tip of each bud carries fifteen to twenty receptors. (7) These receptors are linked by nerve fibers to the brain.

(8) Different areas of the tongue respond to different tastes. (9) For example, the tip of the tongue responds to sweetness. (10) The back of the tongue responds to bitter foods. (11) Therefore, foods containing saccharine taste sweet at first. (12) They trigger a bitter response at the back of the mouth.

(13) Taste is probably caused by a chemical reaction. (14) Molecules of food excite the nerve fiber. (15) The nerve fiber, in turn, sends an impulse to the brain. (16) However, there is more to the process than this. (17) Smell obviously plays an important role. (18) We know, for example, a stuffy nose causes people to lose their sense of taste.

(19) We grow older. (20) The number of taste buds decreases. (21) Children are most sensitive to taste. (22) This may explain their dislike of spicy, savory food.

◆ 18-1 Achieving Sentence Variety

Revise the following passage for sentence variety. Combine three or four pairs of sentences to vary sentence length. Vary some sentence openings so not all sentences begin with the subject. Consider turning one sentence into a question, exclamation, or command to vary sentence type. As you revise, make sure that the relationship between ideas is clear and that you punctuate correctly.

(1) A fossil Tyrannosaurus rex was seized by the FBI. (2) It now belongs to the government. (3) It is one of the best-preserved fossils ever found.

(4) The fossil was uncovered on government land in 1990. (5) The fossil hunters were excited by the find. (6) They sold the fossil to a South Dakota dealer for an unknown amount. (7) The fossil was known as "Sue." (8) It was stored at a private museum in Hill City, South Dakota. (9) Federal agents learned of the fossil's existence. (10) They claimed it was government property because of its original location. (11) A judge agreed. (12) The judge ordered the fossil turned over to the government. (13) Some fossil hunters praised the ruling. (14) Others feared that dealers would stop buying fossils.

(15) The dealer was shocked by the ruling. (16) He plans to sue. (17) This could be the first time a dinosaur visits the Supreme Court.

◆ 18-2 Achieving Sentence Variety

Revise the following passage for sentence variety. Combine sentences to vary sentence length. Vary some sentence openings so not all sentences begin with the subject. Consider turning one sentence into a question, exclamation, or command to vary sentence type. As you revise, make sure that the relationship between ideas is clear and that you punctuate correctly.

(1) Minority groups have grown more vocal in recent years. (2) They have begun to criticize lack of consideration for ethnic history. (3) They have demanded changes in some schools' names, for example. (4) These names honored former slave owners. (5) Few people questioned these names previously. (6) The protesters sparked a debate.

(7) Historical celebrations have also come under fire. (8) Residents of Manatee County in Florida have annually celebrated the Spanish explorer Hernando De Soto. (9) He and his crew killed many Native Americans. (10) The De Soto celebration included a reenactment of his discovery. (11) Townspeople dressed up. (12) They ran through the streets. (13) They waved swords. (14) They screamed "heathen" and "savage." (15) Native Americans protested. (16) The ceremony was toned down.

(17) The question is whether such changes actually do any good. (18) Protesters may alter the names of streets or schools. (19) They do not change the past. (20) The protesters are determined in their beliefs, however. (21) They vow to continue to challenge America's historical focus.

◆ 19-1 Using Parallelism

Edit the following sentences to eliminate faulty parallelism, making any changes you think are needed to maintain parallel structure. If the sentence is correct as written, write *C* in the blank following it.

1. The candidate vowed to fight crime, to lower taxes, and do something about improving education. _____

2. I love you with all my heart, and all my soul, and my being. _____

3. Children who watch more than six hours of television a day tend to have short attention spans, their play is very aggressive, and they also perform poorly in school. _____

4. Citizens can help fight crime by supporting their local police and neighborhood patrols might also be organized. _____

5. In Dr. Davies's American government class, it is as important to take thorough lecture notes as reading every assignment. _____

6. You can stay healthy by watching your diet, you need to get enough rest, and exercising regularly is also important. _____

7. *Consumer Reports* praises this car for its superior design, its low maintenance costs, and it has an excellent resale record. _____

8. My New Year's resolutions were to lose weight, to give up smoking, and to find a new job. _____

9. When she accepted the award, the singer thanked her agent, her husband was waved to, and she took time to praise her parents. _____

10. Some people like Chinese food, while others prefer Italian, and there are still others who most enjoy Mexican. _____

11. Having good health is more important than being rich. _____

12. I enjoy watching basketball more than I would like to watch football. _____

13. To get to the fairgrounds, you can take the subway. Taking the bus is also a possibility. _____

14. Washington and Oregon border the Pacific Ocean. So does California.

15. Sound City not only has a wide selection of audio components but there is also a full line of video equipment sold there. _____

16. Driving without a license deserves a greater fine than it would if you were driving with an expired license. _____

17. New York City is home to the Yankees and the Mets, and the Giants are also a home team. _____

18. Some people say a glass is half empty, while the glass is half full, according to other people. _____

19. Next summer, either I will visit my grandparents in Georgia or I will visit my friends in Chicago. _____

20. The festival always includes circus performers, free music is offered, and there are many different kinds of food. _____

◆ 19-2 Using Parallelism

Edit the following passage to eliminate faulty parallelism, making any changes you think are needed to maintain parallel structure.

(1) A pair of economists recently discovered an interesting thing. (2) Physical attractiveness not only gets people better dates, but a higher income is also a result. (3) Their original study of 7,000 people found that good looks very often meant that a weekly paycheck was bigger. (4) In a follow-up study, the researchers tracked 2,000 students who graduated from law school during the 1970s, who entered legal practice after school, and the practice of law lasted at least fifteen years for them. (5) The results of the new study were surprisingly similar to what the researchers were able to discover in the original study.

(6) There was no relation between class rank at graduation and a student's looks; there was also no relation between what a student's starting salary was and how a student looked. (7) However, after five years on the job, the most attractive graduates earned 9 percent more on average than were the likely earnings for the least attractive graduates. (8) Fifteen years later, the most attractive earned 13 percent more.

(9) The question is whether this is the result of law firms' discriminating against unattractive lawyers, or clients' preferring attractive lawyers is the cause of it. (10) Do unattractive people have a claim to legal protection from discrimination in the workplace? (11) For example, a cosmetics company could not refuse to hire a salesperson based on his or her race, but is it the same thing to refuse to hire a salesperson because of the way he or she looks?

◆ 20-1 Using Words Effectively

For each of the following sentences, fill in the blank with the word in parentheses that is most exact and specific.

1. Sheela received _____ on Valentine's Day. (a gift, choco-

    lates, candy)

2. As the storm approached, the _____ thunder grew louder.

    (booming, sound of, noisy)

3. On the coldest days, I always wear a _____. (warm jacket,

    coat, down parka)

4. The cook threw the meat away because it smelled _____.

    (bad, rancid, really awful)

5. My three-year-old nephew loves to _____ his little toy horn.

    (play, blow on, toot on)

Revise the following sentences to make them more concise, eliminating wordiness, repetition, and overly elevated language.

6. Overweight adolescents who are too heavy may risk serious health problems

    as adults after they mature.

7. It is a fact that the candidates will name their running mates before two weeks

    have had a chance to pass.

8. I have very often entertained the idea that a person's garments are a manner

    or means of nonverbal communication.

9. In this day and age, crime is many people's top, number one concern.

10. When my parents first moved in, their house was originally painted yellow in

    color.

11. Despite the fact that they tried not to think about their daughter's death, the horrible tragedy of the accident never fully left them.

12. Practitioners of the medical profession issue the warning that inhaling the smoke of burning tobacco rolled in white paper has the effect of bringing about unhealthiness.

Consider the effectiveness of the underlined phrases in the following sentences. If a phrase is a fresh, effective simile or metaphor, write *C* in the blank after the sentence. If the phrase is a trite expression, revise it to eliminate the cliché, writing your version in the space above the line.

13. We believe it is time the negotiators <u>laid their cards on the table</u> and worked out an end to the strike. _____

14. The counsellor really <u>hit the nail on the head</u> when she said that our problem is lack of trust in each other. _____

15. A person has to be <u>strong as an ox</u> to get that little lid off an aspirin bottle. _____

16. When he tinkers with his motorcycle, my brother is <u>intent as Dr. Frankenstein making adjustments to his creation.</u> _____

17. When my former boyfriend broke our date to the prom, it was <u>the straw that broke the camel's back.</u> _____

Revise the following sentences to eliminate sexist language.

18. Compassion is a trait that separates man from the animals.

19. Female stockbroker Chris Davidson will offer investment strategies at next week's seminar.

20. Public schools are turning to businessmen in our community for support in offering job training.

◆ 20-2 Using Words Effectively

The following passage contains problems with word choice. Read the passage and evaluate the underlined words and phrases. Cross out any that are not concise or that are trite or clichéd; revise each of these, if necessary, in the space above it. Write *C* above any underlined words or expressions that you do not think need to be corrected. If you wish, add a fresh metaphor or simile to increase the impact of the passage.

(1) I had been attending college in <u>the urban city of</u> Philadelphia for two quarters, <u>which is the equivalent of</u> six months. (2) However, getting used to city life was turning out to be <u>easier said than done</u>.

(3) The crowded streets were <u>not very nice</u> for someone who grew up in a small town, and the <u>stench of hot pretzels mixed with automobile fumes and garbage</u> was <u>unpleasant</u>. (4) Walking to the subway, I <u>stepped around</u> a pile of rags only to realize <u>and come to the conclusion</u> that it was a person <u>lying</u> on the ground, asleep.

(5) When I reached Chestnut Street, I heard a voice <u>saying</u>, "Repent! The Lord is angry! You shall feel His wrath!" (6) It was a man wearing <u>a torn houndstooth jacket, stained polyester pants, one penny loafer, and one high-top sneaker</u>. (7) His hair was grayish yellow <u>in color</u> and <u>looked dirty</u>. (8) He pointed <u>one, single</u> finger at me and began to <u>move</u> in my direction. (9) Feeling as though I was <u>between a rock and a hard place</u>, I stepped off the curb to avoid him, only to hear <u>the sound of a horn</u> and narrowly miss being <u>crushed</u> by a bus. (10) <u>Adding insult to injury</u>, the <u>unusual</u> man said, "Take that as a warning, my friend, because you might have been killed." <u>Despite the fact that</u> I knew I was not deserving of the wrath of heaven, I almost believed him. (11) Could this be <u>the straw that broke the camel's back</u>?

(12) On down the street, I <u>made a transaction for</u> a cheesesteak from a street vendor, which tasted <u>good</u>, and I began to feel better. (13) I stopped to listen to a

saxophonist playing a bluesy number, and <u>it was my feeling at that moment</u> that I had never heard such <u>beautifully spiritual</u> music. (14) A woman <u>of an elderly nature</u> in ragged clothes and <u>thin as a rail</u> also stopped, and I <u>took notice of</u> her <u>eyeing</u> my sandwich. (15) Impulsively, <u>and without thinking</u>, I offered it to her, saying "I can't really eat any more." (16) She smiled and accepted, and I smiled back. (17) For a moment <u>in time</u>, the three of us were connected <u>in that place</u>, and the summer night began to seem <u>pretty as a picture</u>. (18) For the first time, I felt as though the city and I had reached a truce, and I realized <u>in the final analysis</u> that I might learn to like it here.

◆ 21-1 Run-Ons and Comma Splices

Some of the following items contain run-ons or comma splices. Carefully correct the errors, making sure that you clearly indicate the relationship between ideas and that you punctuate correctly. If any sentences are correct as written, put a *C* in the blank following it.

1. The soft drink Seven-Up originally got its name from its ingredients, it is a blend of seven natural flavors, not just lemon and lime. _____

2. Scientists have a theory about the different sizes of our toes they believe the smaller outer toes allow us to balance more effectively. _____

3. A burnt-out lightbulb makes a rattling sound when shaken, the filament has broken, causing the bulb to fail. _____

4. The command *sic*, which is used to instruct a dog to attack, is a variation of the word "seek." _____

5. Most hot dogs today actually don't have skins, however they may seem to because the exterior is firmer than the interior. _____

6. Even plain M & M candies have peanuts in them they are ground up and mixed in with the chocolate. _____

7. The reason the letters *Q* and *Z* are not on a telephone dial is that only twenty-four letters were needed and *Q* and *Z* are the least commonly used letters in English. _____

8. Birds' toes have an amazing locking mechanism allowing them to perch on a branch or wire without falling off, in fact, birds can stand just as easily on one leg as on two. _____

9. No one really knows why we have earlobes, their only function seems to be to hold earrings. _____

10. Blushing is caused by the dilation of blood vessels and the subsequent flow of more blood to the surface of the body. _____

11. The white stuff on baseball card gum is powdered sugar it is sprinkled on to keep the pieces from sticking together. _____

12. Invented in 1885, Dr Pepper is the oldest major soft-drink brand on the market. _____

13. Brown chocolate contains cocoa powder, white chocolate does not. _____

14. A greenish potato chip is completely safe to eat the green tinge comes from chlorophyll. _____

15. Some people believe that the brand name Kodak was chosen because it sounds like a camera shutter clicking, this is not true. _____

16. There is a good reason we take our temperatures with a thermometer in our mouths or other body cavities, the idea is to find out the body's internal temperature. _____

17. The hair of a cat is the most electrostatic of any pet hair this may be why cat hair is so much worse about sticking to our clothing. _____

18. The skin over our elbows is quite wrinkled, while the skin over our knees is much less so. _____

19. Only female mosquitos bite, in fact male mosquitos do not even have a mouth able to pierce skin. _____

20. Milk gets just as cold in a refrigerator as water it just doesn't feel as cold in the mouth. _____

◆ 21-2 Run-Ons and Comma Splices

The following passage contains several run-on sentences and comma splices. Read the passage and circle the number before each run-on and comma splice. Then correct the errors, making sure that the connection between ideas is clear and that the revised sentences are correctly punctuated.

(1) It is well known that some female insects and spiders eat the males during and after mating, the praying mantis and the black widow spider are two examples. (2) Scientists have always believed that the males were eaten because they weren't able to get away. (3) The male, it was assumed, would try to survive to breed again, the female simply considered the male as food. (4) The two were seen as antagonists in a real-life "battle of the sexes."

(5) However, a new discovery seems to cast doubt on this assumption it involves the poisonous redback spider of Australia. (6) During mating, the male redback actually turns over and over, maneuvering himself into a position that makes it easier for the female to eat him. (7) At the same time, the female begins to chew and liquefy the male, then she devours him.

(8) The male offers himself up for sacrifice to his mate in order to ensure the fertilization of the eggs this means that his genes will carry on for another generation. (9) Competition among male redbacks for females is strong, and a male generally has at most one chance to mate. (10) For reasons that remain mysterious, a female who doesn't eat her mate is far less likely to bear his offspring than one who does. (11) The eating ritual does prolong the act of intercourse, this may increase the likelihood of the male's sperm fertilizing the female's eggs. (12) The male may also provide nutrients that increase the devouring female's fertility, therefore she may lay more eggs.

(13) Female redbacks seem to be superior to males in several ways for one thing, the male is only about 2 percent the size of the female. (14) The female is

brightly colored, while the male is drab. (15) The male's adult life lasts only a week or so, females live for up to two years. (16) The male will likely have a chance to mate no more than once, on the other hand, the female can have a number of partners over the course of her life.

(17) One study has shown that a devoured male on average fertilizes twice as many eggs as one who is not eaten. (18) A surviving male even seems to recognize his failure. (19) He remains in the female's web instead of seeking another mate, then he dies within a day or two.

◆ 22-1 Sentence Fragments

The following passage contains several sentence fragments. Read the passage, and circle the number before each fragment. Then correct each fragment by adding the words necessary to complete it or by attaching it to a nearby sentence that completes the idea.

(1) The origin of Valentine's Day is uncertain. (2) Although it certainly dates back more than a thousand years. (3) The holiday honors St. Valentine. (4) A Christian martyr who was supposedly beheaded on February 14 in the year 270. (5) This was the date of an ancient Roman fertility festival, but the early church replaced it. (6) With a feast day honoring St. Valentine. (7) However, the holiday continued to be associated with lovers. (8) By the 1500s, lovers were exchanging tokens of affection on St. Valentine's Day. (9) Such as gloves, garters, and items decorated with hearts and flowers. (10) The 1700s saw the introduction of the Valentine card. (11) Originally, these handmade of paper lace with a handwritten love poem. (12) They might even include a satin heart containing a small present.

(13) Within a hundred years, Valentine cards were being produced commercially. (14) This development leading to a great expansion of the holiday's popularity. (15) These Valentine cards were often very elaborate. (16) And decorated with cupids or flowers. (17) Some card manufacturers began to produce funny and even insulting Valentines. (18) Which continue to be popular today. (19) It is estimated that millions of Valentines are now exchanged every year in the United States alone. (20) This adds up to a billion-dollar business. (21) Including all the candy, flowers, and other gifts that are exchanged, as well.

◆ 22-2 Sentence Fragments

The following passage contains several sentence fragments. Read the passage, and circle the number before each fragment. Then correct each fragment by adding the words necessary to complete it or by attaching it to a nearby sentence that completes the idea.

(1) Many experts in the music industry expecting Tejano to become the United States' next big music sensation. (2) Tejano is a fusion of Latin pop and country and western music. (3) Which is sung with Spanish lyrics. (4) It is a music of the U.S.–Mexican border. (5) Representing the culture of Texas's Hispanic community. (6) Tejano's biggest following now is found in the American Southwest.

(7) However, recording executives expect this style of music eventually to reach a far wider general audience in the United States and Mexico. (8) Partly because its beat is a little bit raunchy but wholesome at the same time. (9) Already one of the recording industry's most profitable specialities.

(10) Tejano came to national media attention after the murder of the singer Selena. (11) Who was on her way to becoming Tejano's first cross-over star. (12) Selena had many adoring fans. (13) In fact, only six months after her death, at least 619 newborn girls had been given her name. (14) In Texas alone. (15) The next big star on the horizon is Emilio Navaira. (16) A singer who is now known simply as Emilio. (17) Emilio has won the male entertainer of the year award at the Tejano Music awards for several years running. (18) And has had several big hits on the Billboard charts. (19) Emilio is popular with Tejano fans for a stage movement called the "Emilio shuffle." (20) He also sings country and western songs in English. (21) Which is unusual for a Tejano musician.

◆ 23-1 Subject-Verb Agreement

For each of the following sentences, decide whether the subject is singular or plural. Then circle the correct present tense verb.

1. The Vietnam Veterans Memorial in Washington, D.C., (honor, honors) men and women killed or missing in the Vietnam War.

2. There (is, are) more than 58,000 names carved into the black granite wall.

3. More than two and a half million people (visit, visits) the site each year.

4. Often, visitors to the Memorial (leave, leaves) mementoes.

5. Each of these (has, have) a special significance.

6. A letter or photograph (is, are) a commonly left memento.

7. Other mementoes that (appear, appears) can include combat boots, stuffed animals, rosaries, and dog tags.

8. A six-pack of beer, along with some flowers, (is, are) the tribute from one soldier every year.

9. One also (find, finds) cigarettes, canned food, and articles of clothing at the Memorial.

10. Family members, buddies, and others (do, does) this to honor the men and women they lost.

11. Parents and others (teach, teaches) children not to make fun of people with a disability.

12. So why (do, does) they see fat people as fair game?

13. Many people (is, are) more than willing to express dislike for the obese.

14. In fact, someone who is fat (seem, seems) to threaten thin people.

15. Perhaps they (see, sees) fat people as something they might become.

16. A fat man or woman (come, comes) to represent laziness, gluttony, and loss of control.

17. Research from the last few years (cast, casts) doubt on these stereotypes, however.

18. Actually, obesity often (has, have) a genetic cause and (is, are) determined by metabolism, not eating.

19. People who (eat, eats) very little can still be fat.

20. Advocates for the obese (believe, believes) it is time to dispel people's fear of fat.

◆ 23-2 Subject-Verb Agreement

The following passage contains several errors in subject-verb agreement. Decide whether each of the underlined verbs agrees with its subject. If it does not, cross it out and write the correct form in the space above. If it does, write *C* above the verb.

(1) Audio books, which <u>is</u> also called books on tape, <u>are</u> only about fifteen years old, but they already <u>earns</u> more than a billion dollars in sales for publishers. (2) One of the largest publishers of audio books <u>has</u> more than one hundred titles in the works each year, and there <u>is</u> many smaller companies also getting in on the act. (3) Best-selling novels and biographies that <u>has</u> been shortened <u>make</u> up most of the market, but literary classics <u>appears</u> to be gaining popularity, as well.

(4) Each of these recordings <u>have</u> to be read, of course. (5) One interesting development relating to audio books <u>is</u> that their production <u>have</u> brought new opportunities for actors. (6) There <u>is</u> several special talents required for readers of audio books. (7) A strong speaking voice, as well as physical endurance, <u>are</u> most important. (8) Also, it <u>do</u> help to have theater training; an actor or actress who <u>have</u> no training <u>is</u> not likely to do well because it can be exhausting to sit for hours reading into a microphone. (9) One executive <u>believes</u> that actors who <u>sings</u> actually <u>makes</u> the best readers because they <u>understands</u> rhythm and phrasing.

(10) Actors with the proper training and ability <u>finds</u> the challenge of recording books rewarding. (11) To actors who <u>has</u> not hit it big, the money they can earn <u>is</u> especially attractive. (12) A fee in the area of $3,500 <u>are</u> usually paid for a two- or three-day session. (13) Another attraction for actors <u>is</u> that one who <u>take</u> on the job of reading <u>get</u> to be the star of the show. (14) He or she <u>does</u> not have to share the stage with other actors and, even better, actually <u>have</u> the chance to play all the characters. (15) <u>Is</u> any actors out there who would miss such an opportunity?

◆ 24-1 Illogical Shifts

Edit the following sentences to eliminate illogical shifts in tense, person, number, discourse, and voice. If any sentences are correct as written, write *C* in the blank.

1. A person who listens to very loud music may damage their hearing. _____

2. The dark clouds and thunder seemed to be getting closer, so we begin to gather up our towels and beach chairs. _____

3. Hollywood's Dorothy Arzner directed the silent film *Fashions for Women* in 1927, and such sound pictures as *Merrily We Go to Hell* and *Dance Girl Dance* were also directed by her. _____

4. Anyone over the age of sixty-five should have your heart checked annually.

    _____

5. A teacher should not have their own children in any class that they teach.

    _____

6. The sign warns people using the pool that you have to be careful when no lifeguard is present. _____

7. The officer asked could she see my driver's license? _____

8. Last year I worked up to fifty hours a week, but this year I am trying to cut back on my hours. _____

9. The play was written by Regina Taylor, and she also starred in its original production. _____

10. Police officers must go through rigorous training before receiving his or her badge. _____

11. My high school English teacher always said that "you are not supposed to end a sentence with preposition." _____

12. College students who work have to budget your time carefully. _____

13. After the second victim was discovered, the detective in the movie decides to take the case. _____

14. A patient who is optimistic about their recovery can generally heal more quickly. _____

15. Healthy dieters eat a lot of protein and carbohydrates, but fats and sweets are avoided by them. _____

16. When the emcee asked were they having a good time, the audience members roared their approval. _____

17. When a woman is pregnant, you should eat nutritiously. _____

18. The lease states that the occupant cannot put any nails in the walls. _____

19. As soon as the dishes were done, in walks Alvin asking if he could help. _____

20. Even though they may not realize it, every child has developed a particular learning style by the age of ten. _____

◆ 24-2 Illogical Shifts

The following passage contains a number of sentences with illogical shifts in tense, person, number, discourse, and voice. Read the passage and circle the number before each sentence containing an illogical shift. Then revise these sentences to eliminate the illogical shifts. Note that some sentences may contain more than one type of illogical shift.

(1) For a recent newspaper article, a reporter asked some experts how will people's eating habits change in the future? (2) One important change is that a person will be more likely to work in their home, and the average business day will also expand to match up with business hours around the world. (3) Consequently, more people will eat takeout meals, and more prepared meals such as pizza will be ordered by them.

(4) One expert says that within ten years people will have diagnostic machines preparing their meals; he predicted that if a person eats too much, these machines will tell you to exercise. (5) Others predict that food will be healthier. (6) Biologists will breed cows to produce lower-fat milk, and leaner pork will also be developed by them. (7) Fat-free frying may become a reality, allowing a fried food lover to enjoy their favorite treats with none of the pound-inducing fat.

(8) Americans in the future are also likely to consume a more international cuisine. (9) In fact, it is common for people today to eat much spicier food than you ate in years past. (10) One expert actually says that "Americans use sixty-eight more spices than they did just ten years ago."

(11) The most frightening prediction concerns the population explosion. (12) If the Earth's human population doubles in the next forty years as some predict, then producing enough food to feed everyone and provide them with adequate nutrition will be a great challenge.

◆ 25-1 Dangling and Misplaced Modifiers

Rewrite the following sentences, which contain dangling and misplaced modifiers, so that each modifier refers to a word or word group it can logically modify.

1. Working at my computer, my eyes started to hurt.

2. Looking carefully at the diamond, its flaws became visible to the dealer.

3. Feeling its way around the dark basement, the mice were finally discovered by the cat.

4. Trying to grab the flying ball, it slipped out of my hand.

5. Frustrated by their low grades, many complaints were heard from the students.

6. Referring to the instructions, the form is easy to fill out.

7. Gathered in the church, I saw the guests waiting for the bride to appear.

8. Mixed with water and sugar, you can create a tasty beverage from cocoa powder.

9. Found on the hospital's doorstep, the baby's parents had abandoned it.

10. Uplifted by the music, a wonderful feeling came over me.

11. Cheryl passed around cookies to everyone on a big tray.

12. My brother drove to meet his girlfriend in his new car.

13. *Jurassic Park* is a novel about dinosaurs who take over the world by Michael Crichton.

14. The novel was turned into a movie following its success.

15. Rubbing his elbow, we watched Glenn grimace in pain from his tennis injury.

16. The dog seemed to be in seventh heaven stretched out in front of the fireplace.

17. Melissa poured the nuts into the bowl mixed in with the pretzels.

18. The hospital workers are demanding more pay with their protests and strikes.

19. With its flowing mane, my sister admired the graceful horse.

20. Running out of his room, Oscar saw the raging fire in his slippers.

◆ 25-2 Dangling and Misplaced Modifiers

The following passage contains some dangling and misplaced modifiers. Read the passage and circle the number before each sentence containing a dangling or misplaced modifier. Then revise these sentences to eliminate the errors. Note that some sentences may contain more than one error.

(1) It is no coincidence that Bill Gates, founder of Microsoft, ranks among the wealthiest individuals in the world. (2) He told a friend that he would be a millionaire by the time he was thirty in the eleventh grade. (3) Having said this, by the age of thirty-one the world saw him become the youngest self-made billionaire ever. (4) The secret of Gates's success is that, while possessing technical insight, he also saw how computers could be used in people's daily lives. (5) Pondering the issue, it became clear to Gates how computer software could be marketed as an indispensable tool for the workplace and home. (6) When Microsoft was founded in 1975, most people had never given computers a thought going about their daily lives. (7) Today, influencing almost every aspect of our lives, many people use computers both at work and at home. (8) Meanwhile, Gates must be thinking of the six billion people inhabiting the globe in their homes and trying to figure out how he can get them all to use Microsoft products. (9) Thinking like a true entrepreneur, the fortune of this man may increase still further.

◆ 26-1 Verbs: Past Tense

In the following sentences, fill in the correct past tense form of each verb in parentheses.

(1) My parents _____ (depart) from Cuba forty years ago. (2) They _____ (start) a new life in Miami. (3) They _____ (select) Miami because my uncle and aunt _____ (live) there. (4) They soon _____ (purchase) a house in Hialeah. (5) That house is where they _____ (raise) me.

For each blank in the paragraph below, fill in the past tense form of the appropriate verb from the following list. Use the verb that makes the best sense in context.

agree	apply	discover	score
start	collect	accept	accuse
receive	cause	believe	
earn	answer	apologize	

(1) Cindy Crawford prides herself on having brains as well as beauty.

(2) Before she _____ high school, her father _____ to pay her $200 if she _____ straight A's all four years. (3) When she _____ her final report card, she _____ her money. (4) While in high school, Crawford _____ to Northwestern University and was _____ into the chemical engineering program. (5) At Northwestern she _____ that her good looks sometimes _____ problems. (6) Professors _____ that because she was pretty, she must also be dumb. (7) For example, a calculus professor _____ her of cheating when she _____ 100 percent on a midterm exam. (8) He eventually _____ for his accusation when she _____ every question correctly on the final, too.

◆ 26-2 Verbs: Past Tense

In the following sentences, fill in the correct past tense form of each verb in parentheses.

1. In 1966, while Dr. Oliver Sacks _____ (be) on the staff of a New York

   hospital, he _____ (come) across some very unusual patients.

2. They _____ (stand) like human statues and never _____ (wake)

   from what _____ (seem) a deep sleep.

3. These patients _____ (have) an unusual disease that doctors

   _____ (know) as sleeping sickness.

4. The disease originally _____ (appear) in Europe early in the century

   and soon _____ (spread) all over the world.

5. It _____ (take) many different forms, and doctors _____ (see)

   a different set of symptoms in each patient.

6. About a third of all victims _____ (die), and others _____ (can)

   not sleep and so _____ (lose) their lives as well.

7. Still others _____ (fall) into a deep coma in which they

   _____ (spend) the rest of their lives.

8. Those who survived _____ (become) almost like zombies and

   _____ (feel) nothing either physically or emotionally.

9. By the late 1920s, only ten years after it _____ (begin), the epidemic

   suddenly _____ (shrink) in proportions and _____ (end).

10. The patients Dr. Sacks discovered _____ (be) long-term survivors

    whom the hospital _____ (keep) isolated in a private ward.

11. The effects of the disease _____ (make) these survivors appear to be living statues.

12. Dr. Sacks _____ (hear) of an experimental drug called L-Dopa that some doctors _____ (use) to treat similar symptoms.

13. He _____ (choose) to experiment with treating these patients with L-Dopa.

14. When he _____ (do), the patients suddenly and almost miraculously _____ (awake).

15. They _____ (bring) their emotions to the surface again, and they _____(think) about the world around them.

16. Many _____ (speak) for the first time in decades, and their voices _____ (ring) through the halls of the ward.

17. They _____ (break) through the barrier that _____ (keep) them from being responsive to anything around them.

18. Ultimately, however, their long illness _____ (cost) them a great deal because they never _____ (grow) beyond the time almost fifty years before when they _____ (catch) the disease.

19. Also, they _____ (will) often experience tics, odd motions, and other bizarre behavior.

20. Most _____ (pass) away in the years following their treatment, but they _____ (teach) doctors much about chemical therapy and _____ (give) new insights into how the human brain works.

◆ 27-1 Verbs: Past Participles

In the following sentences, fill in the correct past participle form of the verbs in parentheses.

1. It has _____ (take) us some time to reach our goals, but our hard

   work has finally _____ (pay) off.

2. In the course of my life, I have _____ (find) that people who have

   _____ (stick) to their principles have _____ (wind) up

   happiest in the long run.

3. My sister has never intentionally _____ (hurt) anyone, yet she has

   often _____ (allow) others to take advantage of her.

4. We have _____ (grow) disillusioned with our political leaders who

   have _____ (keep) almost none of their promises.

5. Some of these politicians have _____ (hold) office for so long that

   they have completely _____ (lose) touch with the average citizen.

6. Experts have _____ (tell) us that the economy has _____

   (improve) over the last few years, but what they have _____ (say)

   does not correspond to our own experience.

7. Others have _____ (lead) us to believe that the country has

   _____ (make) significant gains recently, but we have _____

   (read) between the lines and _____ (notice) that only part of the

   population is affected.

8. Have you _____ (fight) the impulse to become cynical, or have you

   _____ (choose) to ignore what they say?

9. If I had _____ (be) better prepared, I would have _____ (write)

   a longer response to the exam question.

10. If we had _____ (know) that the area was contaminated, we would

   not have _____ (eat) or _____ (drink) anything.

In the following sentences, fill in the tense of the verb in parentheses that makes
the best sense in context. You should use either the present perfect tense or the
past perfect tense.

11. By the time the holidays were over, I _____ _____ (gain) ten

   pounds.

12. Many citizens support Alissa Haggery for election, even though she

   _____ never _____ (hold) public office.

13. The patient _____ _____ (feel) ill for days before he finally

   consented to see a doctor.

14. Since starting my new job last week, I _____ _____ (meet)

   five other employees.

15. The judges believed that the runner _____ _____ (break) a

   record, but they later realized they _____ _____ (make) a

   mistake.

16. It seemed as though I _____ _____ (wait) hours, but in

   reality only a few minutes _____ _____ (pass).

17. China Garden is a great restaurant; I _____ _____ (take) out

   food from there many times, and each time it _____

   _____ (be) delicious.

18. We pretended that we _____ not _____ (see) her the day

   before.

19. I must admit that I _____ _____ (tell) a lie now and then,

   even though I am not proud of the fact.

20. The house _____ _____ (burn) to the ground before the fire

   department arrived.

◆ 27-2 Verbs: Past Participles

The following passage contains several errors in the use of past participles and the perfect tenses. Decide whether each of the underlined verbs or participles is in the correct form. If it is incorrect, cross it out and write the correct form in the space above. If it is correct, write *C* above the verb.

(1) Cooking <u>influence</u> by Latin-American cuisine <u>has began</u> to find great popularity in the United States. (2) As Latin chefs <u>have opened</u> new restaurants and <u>brung</u> new flavors to the eating public, other restaurant owners <u>have chose</u> to experiment with new sauces and seasonings with a Latin flavor. (3) South Americans traditionally <u>have ate</u> dinner later in the evening than people in the United States. (4) Consequently, restaurant owners <u>have found</u> that a Latin-style menu can keep their establishments' tables <u>fill</u> with patrons late into the evening.

(5) Vegetables such as yucca and chayote, which always <u>been</u> staples of Latin cooking, <u>have catch</u> on with non-Latin diners. (6) Perhaps a bit <u>prejudice</u> in favor of native ingredients, Latin chefs <u>have lead</u> the way in bringing new foods to the public. (7) By combining different influences, they <u>have shaken</u> up traditional expectations.

(8) The popularity of Mexican and Southwestern American food <u>had rose</u> in the 1980s, and many believe this movement <u>has pave</u> the way for South American foods. (9) Once diners <u>have become</u> accustomed to the spices <u>use</u> in Mexican foods, they could appreciate the flavors of South America.

(10) As non-Latin chefs <u>have see</u> how popular Latin-style cooking can be, they <u>have turn</u> to their Hispanic staff members for ideas. (11) It <u>has took</u> a while, but respect for Hispanic culture <u>has growed</u> a lot in recent years as more and more non-Hispanic Americans <u>have fell</u> in love with its food.

◆ 28-1 Nouns and Pronouns

In the sentences that follow, circle the correct pronoun in each of the underlined pairs.

1. When we answer the telephone, my father and <u>me/I</u> are often mistaken for each other.

2. <u>Mother-in-laws/Mothers-in-law</u> are often the butt of jokes that are based on unfair stereotypes.

3. I think that either Mariah Carey or Lauryn Hill should win a Grammy for <u>her/their</u> latest recording.

4. The crowd on the street began to try to shove <u>its/their</u> way through the police barricades.

5. If everyone did exactly what <u>he or she/they</u> wanted to, the result would be chaos.

6. We have been working on our term papers for the same amount of time, but Sarita is farther along than <u>I/me</u>.

7. Barry and <u>he/him</u> both play guitar and drums.

8. Our boss divided responsibility for the job between <u>they/them</u> and <u>we/us</u>.

9. All of the <u>children/childrens</u> at the center where I work have had their flu shots.

10. After the victory, the team members congratulated <u>theirselves/themselves</u> on a game well played.

11. During the reunion, each family had <u>its/their</u> portrait taken by a professional photographer.

12. You can have either a free individual pizza or a free hamburger, but <u>they/it</u> must be ordered by 10:00.

13. Each of the portable telephones on the market today comes with <u>their/its</u> own antenna.

14. <u>Her/She</u> and her mother had not seen each other for ten years.

15. Many <u>specieses/species</u> of cockroach are virtually immune to any commercially produced poison.

16. Everyone who wishes to vote must cast <u>their/his or her</u> ballot by the end of the week.

17. Members of the One World organization will be on campus next week so that <u>they/it</u> can provide information about <u>their/its</u> mission.

18. If the decision had been left up to my sister and <u>I/me</u>, we would have had peanut butter for every meal.

19. It took my friend ten minutes longer than <u>I/me</u> to finish the exam.

20. Not even one of the women in my family has ever dyed <u>her/their</u> hair.

◆ 28-2 Nouns and Pronouns

The following passage contains errors in the use of nouns and pronouns. Edit it to eliminate errors in plural noun forms, pronoun case, pronoun-antecedent agreement, and reflexive pronoun forms. Also eliminate nonspecific and unnecessary pronouns.

(1) Last fall, my friend Paul and me volunteered to help out at the Arts Day Festival on the streetes of downtown Sarasota. (2) The festival includes ten different performance sites, and each of these sites has their own line-up of different performances throughout the day. (3) It said in the paper that festival organizers needed people to stage-manage and emcee each site, and us two decided that sounded like fun. (4) We were assigned to a site far from the center of operations, which made Paul and I a little nervous. (5) Our first act was a percussion group, which had to get all their instruments to another site twelve blocks away as soon the second act was to begin. (6) Paul and I, we ran around for twenty minutes trying to find some sort of transportation, but finally the musicians had to carry the drums theirselves, with some help from audience members. (7) Next came a group of circus performers, including childrens and teenagers in a circus training program, as well as professionals from the Center Stage Circus. (8) The audience gave their biggest applause to a team of acrobats and to a hilarious dog act. (9) Every time the dog trainer started a new trick, either a brown poodle or a white terrier would hop down from their stand and jump through a hoop, while the trainer pretended to be upset. (10) The boys and girls in the audience laughed theirselves silly over those two little dogs.

(11) Our next act was a one-man band who had recently been one of the runner-ups in a national competition. (12) He was interrupted, however, by the arrival of the one-hundred-member All County Junior High Honor Band. (13) Each of the five band directors took their turn conducting this group, which seemed to be

playing its very best. (14) Then the one-man band and his singing partner performed their act for the last hour or so.

(15) I don't think any of the other volunteer stage managers had as many different kinds of acts as Paul and me, which made our job a bit challenging. (16) Furthermore, anyone who manages that site next year should make sure that they have plenty of help when it comes time to take down all the folding chairs!

◆ 29-1 Adjectives and Adverbs

In the following sentences, circle the correct adjective or adverb form in each of the underlined pairs.

1. People who help others deserve to feel <u>well/good</u> about themselves.

2. The couple was frozen with fear as the monster approached <u>slow/slowly</u> and <u>steady/steadily</u>.

3. I'm not sure which is <u>worse/worser</u>, to betray a friend or a family member.

4. Whenever the manager is around, the staff treats customers <u>politer/more politely</u>.

5. Sometimes it is <u>real/really</u> difficult for me to keep my mouth shut when I see an animal being treated <u>bad/badly</u>.

6. The magazine article described what it called the <u>finest/most fine</u> collection of Elvis memorabilia in the country.

7. Of all the Presidents in the last sixty years, Ronald Reagan has been considered the <u>more conservative/most conservative</u>.

8. The dancer began moving so <u>wild/wildly</u> that it looked as though she might hurt herself.

9. The candidate looks <u>well/good</u> on television but doesn't speak quite as <u>good/well</u> as the others do.

10. A pair of shoes should fit <u>snug/snugly</u> but not feel too <u>tight/tightly</u>.

11. Taking the ACT test was one of the <u>intensest/most intense</u> experiences of my life.

12. The concert was over much <u>more sooner/sooner</u> than we expected.

13. Will <u>this/these</u> papers be graded by <u>this/these</u> Friday?

14. Of Tower and Video Giant, I've always thought Tower has the <u>better/best</u> selection of tapes.

15. The children can stay only if they play very <u>quiet/quietly</u>.

16. Few things are <u>sweeter/more sweeter</u> than a <u>full/fully</u> ripened tangerine.

17. The scholarship committee seemed <u>favorable/favorably</u> impressed with my answers.

18. The commentator felt the incumbent had done <u>bad/badly</u> in the debate, but we thought he seemed <u>impressive/impressively</u>.

19. I reacted <u>calm/calmly</u> when my best friend started dating my ex, but I had actually never been <u>furiouser/more furious</u> in my life.

20. Of the three routes you can take to get to Houston, this one is <u>shorter/shortest</u>.

◆ 29-2 Adjectives and Adverbs

Edit the following passage to eliminate errors in the use of adjectives and adverbs.

(1) Among the most difficultest environmental problems we face is the effect of gasoline-burning engines on the Earth's atmosphere. (2) Yet, it is real hard to imagine most of the developed world giving up automobiles. (3) Most drivers feel quite suspisciously about attempts to limit the use of cars or to force drivers to use public transportation oftener. (4) Consequently, cars are likely to survive, for better or for worst.

(5) It is likely, however, that cars of the future will become more friendly to the environment. (6) Even within the next ten years, cars will start to undergo some true fundamental changes. (7) For example, a standard car will have two different fuel sources. (8) One will be an internal combustion engine that runs very efficient, getting up to 70 miles per gallon burning an oil-based fuel. (9) However, this engine will be used only to accelerate quick. (10) The system will switch to compressed gas or electricity for cruising speeds, resulting in lesser pollution, which will be well for the environment.

(11) Trains are also expected to become more efficiently and to run more fast. (12) In fact, Amtrak is already in the process of developing the speedier equipment possible, with trains capable of speeds of more than 150 miles an hour. (13) If trains can eventually run this good, perhaps people will be willinger to give up their cars.

◆ 31-1 Using Commas

Add commas to the following sentences as necessary to set off items in series, introductory phrases, transitional words, and appositives, as well as in dates and place names. If any sentences are correct as written, write *C* in the blank.

1. Born in 1844 Sarah Winnemucca Hopkins was an educator a lecturer and a writer. _____

2. Her 1883 biography, *Life among the Paiutes* was one of the earliest published works by a Native American woman. _____

3. A member of the Northern Paiute tribe Winnemucca was born near Humboldt Lake Nevada. _____

4. Her maternal grandfather was leader of the Paiutes living in what later became northeastern California southern Oregon and western Nevada. _____

5. In her biographical work Winnemucca Hopkins records the difficulties faced by the Paiutes when their lands were taken over by white settlers from the East. _____

6. For example the Paiutes were skilled in hunting and fishing. _____

7. U.S. government forces, however confined the tribe to lands that required skill in farming. _____

8. Therefore the tribe almost entirely lost its independence. _____

9. Moreover the tribe's most valuable lands part of the Pyramid Lake Reservation, were robbed by the railroad lines in 1867. _____

10. A skilled linguist Winnemucca became a spokesperson for her people in the 1870s. _____

11. She visited governmental agencies in Carson City, Nevada and San Francisco, California to present her case about the treatment of the Paiutes. _____

12. Her work for her people unfortunately, had little effect. _____

13. In spite of her efforts, the Paiute tribe was forcibly relocated to a reservation near Yakima Washington far from their ancestral lands. _____

14. After marrying a man from Virginia Winnemucca Hopkins moved with him to Boston. _____

15. With the support of several prominent women in the community she began to lecture throughout the Northeast. _____

16. Her subjects were the unfair treatment of Native American people, the difficulty of life on reservations and the need for changes in U.S. government policies. _____

17. A highly controversial figure she was often criticized in the press. _____

18. She felt nevertheless, that it was necessary to bring public attention to the wrongs suffered by native peoples. _____

19. Late in her life, she started the Peabody School the first educational institution for Native Americans run by Native Americans. _____

20. She died on October 17 1891 while visiting her sister and is buried in Henry Lake Montana. _____

◆ 31-2 Using Commas

Add commas as necessary in the following passage to set off items in series, introductory phrases, transitional words, and appositives.

(1) The tropical rainforests are home to some of the most amazing creatures in the world. (2) The habitat of the golden toads for example, is a single square-mile of mountaintop in the rainforest of Costa Rica the only place on Earth where they are found. (3) In addition the basilisk lizard is found inside the rainforest. (4) Amazingly enough this lizard can actually run on the surface of the water from one side of a pond to the other. (5) Among the most beautiful birds in the world male quetzals are also dependent on their rainforest habitat. (6) Neither the golden toad the basilisk nor the quetzal can survive outside the rainforest. (7) To preserve them we must work to preserve their habitat.

(8) In addition to such animals tropical plants in the rainforests provide the main compounds in many drugs. (9) Quinine for instance is extracted from the cinchona tree a native of the rainforest. (10) Quinine is essential for the treatment of malaria a disease that kills more than a million people in Africa every year. (11) With the destruction of the rainforest this important cure for malaria might be lost. (12) The rosy periwinkle another rainforest native is also endangered; two drugs derived from this plant are used in the fight against cancer. (13) Medicines from other rainforest plants are used to treat ulcer problems heart problems and infections. (14) In fact medical research about cures for many diseases focuses on species from the rainforest. (15) More than 80,000 plants throughout the rainforest have yet to be tested for their effectiveness in cancer treatment for example. (16) Already endangered many of these plants may never have a chance to be tested as potential cures.

◆ 32-1 Using Apostrophes

Edit the following sentences to eliminate errors in the use of apostrophes. Look for apostrophes that need to be added, deleted, or repositioned. If any sentences are correct as written, write *C* in the blank.

1. This brochure explains your colleges admissions policies. _____

2. Some movie stars' careers' did not start so brightly. _____

3. One famous actor supported himself for years by selling womens' shoes. _____

4. The players were concerned because Coach Brown did'nt show up for practice. _____

5. Many parents child-care problems will be solved by the new center. _____

6. Warmed by the sun's rays, the dog began to wag it's tail. _____

7. It's odd, I know, but I can never remember that jokes' punchline. _____

8. We must strive to protect all childrens' rights and to ensure that their's is a happy future. _____

9. Doctor's have discovered that this tree's bark may hold a cure for cancer. _____

10. The childrens clinic is open six days a week. _____

11. The firefighter's union is threatening a strike. _____

12. Some people think Aretha Franklins greatest recording is "Respect." _____

13. Is that opinion the same as yours? _____

14. Students have complained about the smell in the library, but so far their complaints havent done much good. _____

15. Three workers lost their lives when the factory exploded. _____

16. Many parents are calling for that principals' resignation. _____

17. A homeless persons greatest enemy is the indifference of other's. _____

18. A single act of kindness can make a big difference in many peoples' lives. _____

19. Last year, the hockey team had it's best season ever. _____

20. The Kramdens upstairs neighbors and best friends' are the Nortons. _____

◆ 32-2 Using Apostrophes

Edit the following passage to eliminate errors in the use of apostrophes. Look for apostrophes that need to be added, deleted, or repositioned.

(1) When you share a pizza with someone, your friends way of tasting it may be very different from your's. (2) Tastes vary because peoples' tongues have different numbers of taste buds. (3) Although scientists have known about genetic taste differences for years, theyve only recently discovered that some people actually have many more taste buds' than other people do. (4) These supertasters tongues have up to one hundred times more taste buds than a nontasters tongue. (5) When a nontaster eats a particular food, it's taste may be almost nonexistent. (6) Supertasters, however, will taste the same food quite intensely because theres a greater number of taste buds in their mouths to be stimulated. (7) These wide differences in tasting ability account for a foods acceptance or lack of acceptance by different people. (8) In a recent experiment, for example, some childrens' responses to cheddar cheese were tested. (9) Most of the supertasters in the group didnt like it. (10) The nontasters, however, liked it very much. (11) Researchers were not surprised by the supertasters' response to the cheese because its' ingredients include some elements that are especially bitter to such tasters.

(12) Interestingly, a womans chance of being a supertaster is much greater than that of a man. (13) In fact, some researcher's findings show that two-thirds of those identified as supertasters are women. (14) Another discovery is that women tend to find intensely sweet flavors unpleasant, while its just the opposite for men. (15) Womens' dislike for sweet tastes may be genetic, although one researcher thinks it may have more to do with the fear of gaining weight. (16) If researchers are correct, theres probably a genetic link between alcoholism and taste buds, too. (17) Because children who's parents are alcoholics are often nontasters, there seems

to be a direct connection between the two. (18) A nontasters ability to drink considerable quantities of alcohol may be due in part to the fact that the nontaster does'nt experience alcohol as being so bitter as others do. (19) With an awareness of these different tasters existence, a food company may do well to reconsider it's marketing strategies.

◆ 33-1 Understanding Mechanics

Edit the following sentences to eliminate errors in capitalization of common and proper nouns, punctuation of direct quotations, and title format. If any sentences are correct as written, write *C* in the blank.

1. The researcher from Stanford university said, "the experiment is a success."

   _____

2. As my best Friend Deanice always says, what goes around, comes around.

   _____

3. At the end of the short story the lottery, Mrs. hutchinson screams it isn't fair, it isn't right. _____

4. Actress Cicely Tyson won an emmy for the television movie the autobiography of miss jane pittman, and she was nominated for an oscar for the theatrical movie sounder. _____

5. An article in the magazine Christopher Street quotes model Christy Turlington as saying, we definitely have great strength being women. _____

6. The class president reminded the graduating Seniors of Rosemont high school that they had to return their caps and gowns by friday afternoon. _____

7. When judge Allanson asked whether the witness was prejudiced against latino and asian-american citizens, the defense attorney shouted, "I object"! _____

8. When Rashaad Salaam accepted his heisman trophy, he said that the Position Coach at colorado state deserved his special thanks. _____

9. The monster in Mary Shelley's novel frankenstein laments, everywhere, I see bliss from which I alone am irrevocably excluded. _____

10. Politicians in washington, d.c., must certainly be glad that in the movie Dirty Harry Clint Eastwood said go ahead, make my day. _____

11. The Guinness book of world records notes that the largest inhabited castle in the World is Windsor castle at Windsor in great britain. _____

12. In 1648, king charles II granted a three-year charter to the first Union in the United states, which was named the shoemakers and booters union. _____

13. Gwendolyn Brooks's poem a Song in the front yard begins with the line I've stayed in the front yard all my life. _____

14. Singer sonja marie performed the song and i gave my love to you on the soundtrack of the movie waiting to exhale. _____

15. "In spite of everything, wrote Anne Frank, I still believe that people are really good at heart. _____

16. In his book "Do Penguins have knees?," David Feldman asks why is our mathematical vocabulary a seemingly random hodgepodge of greek and latin terminology? _____

17. The statue of Liberty stands on ellis island in the Harbor of New York city.

    _____

18. A doctor must earn a medical degree and pass state boards before being allowed to set up a practice, according to the publication *Know Your Rights as a Patient*. _____

19. Remove paper before loading warns the label on my new hewlett packard brand printer. _____

20. The washington post recently broke a story about plots to bomb the offices of the federal aviation commission and the world watch organization. _____

◆ 33-2 Understanding Mechanics

Edit the following passage to eliminate errors in capitalization of common and proper nouns, punctuation of direct quotations, and title format.

(1) Singer and Actress Ethel waters was the first african-american woman to become an entertainment star in the United states. (2) She was born to a poor Family in Chester, pennsylvania, in 1896. (3) As a young woman, she worked as a chambermaid before achieving the beginnings of success in Show Business at seventeen, performing under the name sweet mama stringbean. (4) An accomplished blues singer, she had hits with such popular songs as <u>Dinah</u> and <u>stormy weather</u>, and she was particularly associated with the hymn "His eye is on the sparrow."

(5) On broadway, she starred in a number of popular musicals, including "As thousands cheer" and "cabin in the sky." (6) She also appeared in the metro-goldwyn-mayer film version of "cabin in the sky," about which the magazine Variety wrote whatever its box office fate, it is a worthwhile picture for Metro to have made, if only as a step toward hollywood recognition of the place of the black man in American Life. (7) Waters's greatest Triumph was as the character Berenice sadie Brown in the play Member of the Wedding, a role she repeated in the film version. (8) Set in a small georgia town, it is the story of a lonely twelve-year-old girl and the compassionate housekeeper who looks after her. (9) Among her other films is "pinky," for which she received an Academy award nomination. (10) She also published two volumes of autobiography, including the best-selling To me it's wonderful.

(11) An active member of the national association for the advancement of colored people, Waters was instrumental in opening the way for black performers who followed her.

◆ 34-1 Understanding Spelling

Edit the following sentences to eliminate spelling errors. Decide whether each underlined word is spelled correctly or incorrectly. If the word is misspelled, correct it in the space above. If the spelling given is correct, write *C* above the word.

1. It was the <u>nineth</u> time in two weeks that I had been <u>annoied</u> by my <u>neighbors'</u> yapping dog.

2. The class was <u>suppose</u> to begin at 10 o'clock, but the instructor was <u>quit</u> late.

3. It is difficult to <u>here</u> a <u>piece</u> of music when <u>its</u> being played on poor equipment.

4. I was <u>hopeing</u> to <u>achieve</u> an A on the test, but a B was better <u>then</u> nothing.

5. Sometimes it feels as though <u>were</u> being <u>decieved</u> by politicians on a <u>dayly</u> basis.

6. Under cross-examination, the witness <u>admited</u> that <u>there</u> had been some <u>overeaction</u> on the part of the police officer.

7. After the <u>twentieth</u> of the month, it is <u>to</u> late to drop a class; you must complete the paperwork before the October <u>brake</u>.

8. When you <u>loose</u> a game, you may <u>fine</u> yourself feeling depressed.

9. <u>Niether</u> the <u>principal</u> nor the counsellors knew <u>definitly</u> when the test would be administered.

10. <u>Weather</u> your <u>busyness</u> is a small card shop or a giant manufacturing corporation, it takes sound <u>judgement</u> to succeed.

11. In the <u>past</u>, people who <u>traped</u> animals did so for food, not for sport.

12. Becoming a full <u>professer</u> at a college <u>used</u> to be the norm, but today it is <u>dependant</u> on many factors.

13. There has been a <u>noticable</u> drop in the number of endangered <u>species</u> <u>displaid</u> in most zoos.

14. I was <u>truely</u> <u>supprised</u> at the number of applicants <u>whose</u> resumes contained <u>mispellings</u>.

15. A <u>continuous</u> stream of customers <u>past</u> <u>threw</u> the doors.

16. If <u>your</u> planning to attend the concert, you'd better get tickets <u>right</u> away.

17. When people have strong <u>beleifs</u>, it doesn't matter how <u>inteligent</u> they are; they will probably ignore rational <u>arguements</u>.

18. It <u>occurred</u> to me <u>to</u> late that I needed to <u>develope</u> a better attitude toward school.

19. A cute puppy may be <u>appealling</u>, but it should be <u>plain</u> that owning a dog is a big <u>responsability</u>.

20. She <u>knew</u> the <u>affects</u> of secondhand cigarette smoke, so she kept her smoking <u>seperate</u> from her loved ones.

◆ 34-2 Understanding Spelling

Edit the following passage to eliminate spelling errors. Correct each misspelled word in the space above it.

(1) Most all of us reconize that we can perceive alot about people by reading the expressions on their faces. (2) However, it is also possable to understand people by refering to there body language.

(3) For example, it will often be plane when a person is telling a lie because he or she will fidget a bit. (4) The most common gesture indicateing a lie is touching the head in some way. (5) Rubbing the back of the neck usully suggests that one is truely uncertain of what one is saying. (6) Rubbing one's eye or nose can be an unconscience way of covering the decieving words comming out of one's mouth. (7) This does not mean that you should always disbelieve someone who's every day gestures sometimes include touching the face. (8) However, when you are uncertain weather to trust someone's words, you may want to wiegh the importance of they're gestures.

(9) Observeing how people sit, stand, and move on social occassions can also be informative. (10) People who stand with their arms and legs crossed are generly feeling somwhat defensive or closed. (11) A hand on the hip suggests confidence, while scratching one's arm or leg may indicate insecureity. (12) A person who sets as part of a group with his or her arms crossed and legs pointed away from the others is likly to be feeling withdrawn from the conversation, or at least witholding judgment. (13) One who reclines a bit with his or her hands behind the head is probly quit confident and perhaps even feeling superior to the rest of the group. (14) Two people who are close freinds and very use to each other's company will often position themselves on a couch so that they are turned slightly but noticably toward each other. (15) They may even adopt a very simular posture.

(16) While judgeing people by their body language has obvious limitations, it can also be of benifit as a way of geting to no other people.

Answers

Sentence Skills Diagnostic Test

	Answer	Skill or problem	Book chapter	Exercise Central exercises	Writing Guide Software tutorial
1.	a	sentence fragments	22	Ch. 22, #s 15–16	✓
2.	a	subject-verb agreement	23	Ch. 23, #s 17–20	✓
3.	a	illogical shifts	24	Ch. 24, #s 21–23	✓
4.	a	dangling and misplaced modifiers	25	Ch. 25, #s 24–27	✓
5.	b	verbs: past tense	26	Ch. 26, #s 28–31	✓
6.	c	nouns and pronouns	28	Ch. 28, #s 36–42	✓
7.	a	adjectives and adverbs	29	Ch. 29, #s 43–46	✓
8.	a	ESL issues	30	Ch. 30, #s 47–55	
9.	a	commas	31	Ch. 31, #s 56–62	✓
10.	a	apostrophes	32	Ch. 32, # 63	✓
11.	b	parallelism	19	Ch. 19, #s 10–11	✓
12.	a	run-ons and comma splices	21	Ch. 21, #s 13–14	✓
13.	b	ESL issues	30	Ch. 30, #s 47–55	

	Answer	Skill or problem	Book chapter	Exercise Central exercises	Writing Guide Software tutorial
14.	c	illogical shifts	24	Ch. 24, #s 21–23	✓
15.	a	subject-verb agreement	23	Ch. 23, #s 17–20	✓
16.	c	commas	31	Ch. 31, #s 56–62	✓
17.	b	mechanics	33	Ch. 33, #s 64–67	
18.	b	parallelism	19	Ch. 19, #s 10–11	✓
19.	b	ESL issues	30	Ch. 30, #s 47–55	
20.	a	apostrophes	32	Ch. 32, # 63	✓
21.	b	run-ons and comma splices	21	Ch. 21, #s 13–14	✓
22.	b	sentence fragments	22	Ch. 22, #s 15–16	✓
23.	a	illogical shifts	24	Ch. 24, #s 21–23	✓
24.	c	verbs: past tense	26	Ch. 26, #s 28–31	✓
25.	a	nouns and pronouns	28	Ch. 28, #s 36–42	✓
26.	a	adjectives and adverbs	29	Ch. 29, #s 43–46	✓
27.	b	verbs: past participles	27	Ch. 27, #s 32–35	✓
28.	c	ESL issues	30	Ch. 30, #s 47–55	
29.	c	parallelism	19	Ch. 19, #s 10–11	✓
30.	c	subject-verb agreement	23	Ch. 23, #s 17–20	✓

	Answer	Skill or problem	Book chapter	Exercise Central exercises	Writing Guide Software tutorial
31.	c	commas	31	Ch. 31, #s 56–62	✓
32.	b	mechanics	33	Ch. 33, #s 64–67	
33.	c	run-ons and comma splices	21	Ch. 21, #s 13–14	✓
34.	c	illogical shifts	24	Ch. 24, #s 21–23	✓
35.	b	sentence fragments	22	Ch. 22, #s 15–16	✓
36.	a	verbs: past tense	26	Ch. 26, #s 28–31	✓
37.	b	nouns and pronouns	28	Ch. 28, #s 36–42	✓
38.	a	ESL issues	30	Ch. 30, #s 47–55	
39.	a	commas	31	Ch. 31, #s 56–62	✓
40.	a	subject-verb agreement	23	Ch. 23, #s 17–20	✓
41.	b	dangling and misplaced modifiers	25	Ch. 25, #s 24–27	✓
42.	c	verbs: past participles	27	Ch. 27, #s 32–35	✓
43.	b	ESL issues	30	Ch. 30, #s 47–55	
44.	c	nouns and pronouns	28	Ch. 28, #s 36–42	✓
45.	c	ESL issues	30	Ch. 30, #s 47–55	
46.	b	adjectives and adverbs	29	Ch. 29, #s 43–46	✓
47.	c	illogical shifts	24	Ch. 24, #s 21–23	✓

	Answer	Skill or problem	Book chapter	Exercise Central exercises	Writing Guide Software tutorial
48.	b	subject-verb agreement	23	Ch. 23, #s 17–20	✓
49.	a	dangling and misplaced modifiers	25	Ch. 25, #s 24–27	✓
50.	c	ESL issues	30	Ch. 30, #s 47–55	

◆ 15-1 Writing Simple Sentences

1. (During halftime,) the coach [S] gave [AV] the players a pep talk.

2. Mushrooms and anchovies [S] are [LV] my least favorite pizza toppings.

3. A huge branch [S] from an oak tree crashed [AV] (through the picture window) (during the storm.)

4. (By the next day,) the little girl [S] (with the broken arm) was feeling [LV] better.

5. The director [S] (of the movie) took [AV] more than half an hour setting up the shot.

6. (On Broadway,) the Delaney sisters [S] were portrayed [AV] in the play *Having Our Say.*

7. Thunder and lightning [S] can frighten [AV] young children.

8. Some adults [S] are [LV] allergic (to cats and dogs.)

9. (For someone) (in my position,) the most difficult part [S] (of the job) is [AV] the hours.

10. (With computer networks,) people [S] can have [AV] long conversations (without ever speaking) (to each other.)

11. (From time to time,) each [S] (of us) needs [AV] a helping hand.

12. Jay Leno [S] has been hosting [AV] the *Tonight* show (for some years now.)

13. Jay and David Letterman [S] are [LV] rivals (in the late-night spot.)

14. A special celebration [S] is being planned [AV] (for his tenth anniversary.)

15. (Next week,) a hot new club [S] is opening [AV] downtown.

16. We [S] have already received [AV] our invitations.

17. Have you and your brothers [S] received [AV] your invitations yet?

18. Someone [S] (in town) has been spreading [AV] rumors (about the Cruises.)

19. A tropical storm (of great force) is headed (toward the Caribbean.)

20. Forecasters predict a great deal (of damage.)

◆ 15-2 Writing Simple Sentences

1. The average cow spends eighteen hours a day chewing.

2. (In Washington, D.C.,) any new building must be shorter than the Capitol.

3. The tombstone (of the founder) (of Borden's Dairy) was designed (in the shape) (of a can of condensed milk.)

4. Honeybees and turtles have no sense (of hearing.)

5. Former President Jimmy Carter once rolled his feet (over soda bottles.)

6. (On average,) a person (in the United States) can expect almost one hundred fifty colds (in a lifetime.)

7. (In Arabic,) the word *sheik* means "old man."

8. Every home team (in the National League) must provide the referee (with twenty-four footballs) (for each game.)

9. Ducks sometimes sleep while swimming.

10. Many more radios have been sold (in the United States) than televisions.

11. (According to an ancient Hindu law,) adulterers were punished (by the removal) (of their noses.)

12. A flamingo can only eat (with its head upside down.)

13. Almost half (of the bones) (in one's body) are (in one's hands and feet.)

14. Ping-pong balls have been clocked (at more than one hundred miles an hour.)

15. Portraits (of living people) are prohibited (on U.S. postage stamps.)

16. (In 1944,) Fidel Castro was voted Cuba's top student athlete.

17. The word *typewriter* can be typed (on the top line) (of letters) (of a typewriter keyboard.)

18. King Juan Carlos (of Spain) was killed accidentally (by his brother) (with an air rifle.)

19. Chinese folding money was first made (of deerskin.)

20. (In 1980,) Carolyn Farrell (of Dubuque, Iowa,) became the first nun mayor (of an American city.)

◆ 16-1   Writing Compound Sentences

Other correct answers are possible.

1. Speech is silver, but silence is golden.

2. The house was dark, so she decided not to ring the doorbell.

3. He signed a long-term contract, for he did not want to lose the job.

4. They will not surrender, nor will they agree to a cease-fire.

5. They might leave in the morning, or they might wait until tomorrow afternoon.

6. She had lived in California for many years, but she remembered her Kansas childhood clearly.

7. Melody dropped French, and then she added Spanish.

8. The star witness changed his testimony, so the defendant was acquitted.

9. There are thirty applicants for the program, but only ten will be admitted.

10. Everything seemed different, but nothing had really changed at all.

11. The movie won many awards; however, it didn't make money at the box office.

12. The weather was cold and drizzly; therefore, the outdoor festival was not a success.

13. My father comes from a large family; in fact, he is the fifth of thirteen children.

14. Earth Sciences 101 has both day and evening sessions; however, Anthropology 101 is only offered at night.

15. The experimental drug has several side effects; for example, it may cause nausea in some patients.

16. The new mall provides many opportunities for shopping; in addition, it offers a food court with seven different vendors.

17. The speed limit sign was illegible; nevertheless, the officer gave me a ticket for speeding.

18. I had never been through customs before; consequently, I didn't know what to expect.

19. People often complain about the quality of television programming; however, they continue to watch.

20. Most fast food is very high in fat and calories; in fact, one serving of french fries has more than ten grams of fat.

◆ 16-2 Writing Compound Sentences

Other correct answers are possible.

a.   (1) Children in the United States do not eat enough fruits and vegetables/; (2) ~~They~~ *in fact, they*

average only about half the recommended daily serving. (3) Parents may want to get their

children to eat fruits and vegetables/, (4) ~~They~~ *but they* don't know how. (5) Following are a few basic

steps for doing so.

     (6) A family can begin with breakfast. (7) Cereal can be topped with bananas or berries/,

(8) ~~F~~*or f*ruit juice can be served. (9) Vegetables are good for snack time/; (10) ~~Cut-up~~ *for example, cut-up* carrots can

be served with a flavorful dip. (11) Sandwiches can also be a way of adding vegetables.

(12) Tuna salad is good with celery, pepper slices, and bean sprouts/; (13) ~~A~~ *a* turkey sandwich

can include cucumber, lettuce, and tomato.

     (14) As a treat, fruit can be dipped in chocolate. (15) Children can enjoy it like candy/,

but t
(16) ~~T~~hey still get the added nutritional benefits of fresh fruit.

b.   (1) Everyone complains about the weather sometimes/; (2) ~~M~~*however, m*ost people actually live

where the climate is fairly moderate. (3) Some locales on Earth offer truly extreme

and s
temperatures/, (4) ~~S~~ome places are barely habitable by humans.

     (5) One area difficult for human existence is the Arctic region. (6) Temperatures go as

low as 70 degrees below zero and remain below freezing most of the year. (7) Such intense

but i
cold discourages human habitation/, (8) ~~I~~ntense heat is just as discouraging. (9) Deserts can

for example, t
be impossibly hot/; (10) ~~T~~he Sahara in Africa reaches ground temperatures of up to

and t
150 degrees. (11) There may be no rain for years at a time/, (12) ~~T~~he air becomes too dry for

people to breathe safely.

     (13) The driest place on Earth is the Atacama desert in Chile. (14) Cold atmospheric

so v
currents and high surrounding mountains form a barrier to rain clouds/, (15) ~~V~~ery little rain

falls. (16) In fact, no rain has ever been recorded in some areas of the Atacama.

1. After the sun set, the sky changed to a deep, starry blue.

2. The band warmed up for half an hour before the concert began.

3. The car crashed into the wall as passersby watched helplessly.

4. I support the president although I don't always agree with his decisions.

5. It was almost midnight when my son finally walked through the door.

6. I decided to spend the night because it was too late to drive home.

7. After all the votes were counted, our candidate won.

8. My grandmother worked as a nurse for thirty years until she retired and started a restaurant.

9. Since Melanie started working for the company six months ago, she has already been promoted twice.

10. The class was moved to a larger room so that everyone would have a seat.

11. Martin Luther King Jr. wrote the book *Why We Can't Wait*, which expresses his views on civil rights.

12. Edward Teach, who was also known as Blackbeard the Pirate, was infamous for his cruelty.

13. Black Hawk, who was chief of the Sauk and Fox Indians, refused to move west of the Mississippi.

14. The International Workers of the World was an early labor organization that recruited both skilled and unskilled labor.

15. *Citizen Kane* is a classic movie in which Orson Welles plays an egomaniacal newspaper publisher.

16. Prozac is a prescription drug that is used in treating depression.

17. Stephen King is one of America's most popular writers whose books are often made into successful movies.

18. The actor Paul Robeson, who played many important black roles, was the victim of much discrimination in the United States.

19. Ida Lupino, who starred in dozens of movies in the 1940s and 1950s, was proudest of her career as a director.

20. The Sundance Institute, which was founded by Robert Redford, supports the work of young, independent film directors.

◆ 17-2 Writing Complex Sentences

Other correct answers are possible.

(1) ~~The~~ *Although the* sense of taste is known to everyone, (2) *E*xactly how we taste is not so well understood. (3) Taste is detected by tiny, barrel-shaped taste buds. (4) Most of these are located on the upper surface of the tongue, (5) *although a* few are further down in the throat. (6) The tip of each bud carries fifteen to twenty receptors, (7) ~~These receptors~~ *that* are linked by nerve fibers to the brain.

(8) Different areas of the tongue respond to different tastes. (9) For example, the tip of the tongue responds to sweetness, (10) ~~The~~ *while the* back of the tongue responds to bitter foods. (11) Therefore, foods containing saccharine taste sweet at first, (12) ~~They~~ *before they* trigger a bitter response at the back of the mouth.

(13) Taste is probably caused by a chemical reaction. (14) *When m*Molecules of food excite the nerve fiber, (15) ~~The nerve fiber~~ *it,* in turn, sends an impulse to the brain. (16) However, there is more to the process than this, (17) *because s*Smell obviously plays an important role. (18) We know, for example, a stuffy nose causes people to lose their sense of taste.

(19) *As w*We grow older, (20) *t*The number of taste buds decreases. (21) Children are most sensitive to taste, (22) ~~This~~ *which* may explain their dislike of spicy, savory food.

◆ 18-1 Achieving Sentence Variety

Other correct answers are possible.

(1) A fossil Tyrannosaurus rex, *which* was seized by the FBI, (2) *It* now belongs to the government. (3) It is one of the best-preserved fossils ever found.

(4) The fossil was uncovered on government land in 1990. (5) The fossil hunters were excited by the find, (6) ~~They~~ *and* sold the fossil to a South Dakota dealer for an unknown amount. (7) ~~The fossil was~~ *K*Known as "Sue," (8) *the fossil*It was stored at a private museum in Hill City, South Dakota. (9) *When federal*Federal agents learned of the fossil's existence, (10) *t*They claimed it was government property because of its original location. (11) A judge agreed, (12) ~~The~~ *and*

judge ordered the fossil turned over to the government. (13) Some fossil hunters praised the

~~ruling~~, (14) ~~Ø~~thers feared that dealers would stop buying fossils. *while o*

     (15) ~~The dealer was~~ ~~s~~hocked by the ruling, (16) ~~He~~ plans to sue. (17) ~~This could~~ be the *the dealer* *Could this*

first time a dinosaur visits the Supreme Court.?

◆ 18-2 Achieving Sentence Variety

Other correct answers are possible.

     (1) ~~M~~inority groups have grown more vocal in recent years, (2) ~~T~~hey have begun to *As m* *t*

criticize lack of consideration for ethnic history. (3) ~~They~~ have demanded changes in some *For example, they*

schools' names, ~~for example.~~ (4) ~~These names~~ honored former slave owners. (5) ~~F~~ew people *that* *Because f*

questioned these names previously, (6) ~~T~~he protesters sparked a debate. *t*

     (7) Historical celebrations have also come under fire. (8) Residents of Manatee County

in Florida have annually celebrated the Spanish explorer Hernando De Soto, (9) ~~He~~ and his *even though he*

crew killed many Native Americans. (10) The De Soto celebration included a reenactment of

his discovery. (11) Townspeople dressed up, (12) ~~They~~ ran through the streets, (13) ~~They~~ *and*

wav~~ed~~ swords, (14) ~~They~~ scream~~ed~~ "heathen" and "savage." (15) Native Americans *ing* *and* *ing* *When*

protested, (16) ~~T~~he ceremony was toned down. *t*

     (17) ~~The question is whether~~ such changes actually do any good.? (18) Protesters may *Do*

alter the names of streets or schools, (19) ~~T~~hey do not change the past. (20) ~~The~~ protesters *but t* *However, the*

are determined in their beliefs, ~~however.~~ (21) ~~They~~ vow to continue to challenge America's *and*

historical focus.

◆ 19-1 Using Parallelism

Other correct answers are possible.

1. The candidate vowed to fight crime, to lower taxes, and ~~do something about~~ improv~~ing~~ *to* *e*

    education. _____

2. I love you with all my heart, and all my soul, and ^ my being. _____ *all*

3. Children who watch more than six hours of television a day tend to have short attention

    spans, ~~their~~ play ~~is~~ very aggressive ^, and ~~they also~~ perform poorly in school. _____ *to* *ly* *to*

4. Citizens can help fight crime by supporting their local police and ~~might also be organized~~ neighborhood patrols ^organizing^ _____

5. In Dr. Davies's American government class, it is as important to take thorough lecture notes as ^to^ reading every assignment. _____

6. You can stay healthy by watching your diet, ~~you need to get~~ ^getting^ enough rest, and exercising regularly ~~is also important~~. _____

7. *Consumer Reports* praises this car for its superior design, its low maintenance costs, and ~~it has~~ ^its^ an excellent resale record. _____

8. My New Year's resolutions were to lose weight, to give up smoking, and to find a new job. ___C___

9. When she accepted the award, the singer thanked her agent, her husband, ~~was waved to,~~ ^waved to^ and ~~she took time to~~ praise^d^ her parents. _____

10. Some people like Chinese food, ~~while~~ others prefer Italian, and ~~there are~~ still others ~~who~~ most enjoy Mexican. _____

11. ~~Having good~~ ^Being^ health^y^ is more important than being rich. _____

12. I enjoy watching basketball more than ~~I would like to~~ watch^ing^ football. _____

13. To get to the fairgrounds, you can take the subway, ^or^ ~~Taking~~ the bus ~~is also a possibility~~. _____

14. Washington, ~~and~~ Oregon, ^and California^ border the Pacific Ocean. ~~So does California.~~ _____

15. Sound City not only has a wide selection of audio components but ~~there is~~ ^has^ also a full line of video equipment ~~sold there~~. _____

16. Driving without a license deserves a greater fine than ~~it would if you~~ were driving with an expired license. _____

17. New York City is home to the Yankees, ~~and~~ the Mets, and the Giants^,^ ~~are also a home team~~. _____

18. Some people say a glass is half empty, while ^other say the glass is half full~~/. according to other~~

    ~~people.~~ _____

19. Next summer, either I will visit my grandparents in Georgia or I will visit my friends in

    Chicago. __C__

20. The festival always includes circus performers, free music~~,~~ , ~~is offered~~, and ~~there are~~

    many different kinds of food. _____

◆ 19-2 Using Parallelism

Other correct answers are possible.

(1) A pair of economists recently discovered an interesting thing. (2) Physical
attractiveness not only gets people better dates, but ^*it also gets them* a higher income. ~~is also a result.~~
(3) Their original study of 7,000 people found that good looks very often meant ~~that~~ a ^*bigger* weekly

paycheck. ~~was bigger.~~ (4) In a follow-up study, the researchers tracked 2,000 students who

graduated from law school during the 1970s, ~~who~~ entered legal practice after school~~/~~ and ~~the~~

practice ^*d* ~~of~~ law ~~lasted~~ at least fifteen years. ~~for them.~~ (5) The results of the new study were
surprisingly similar to ^*those of* ~~what the researchers were able to discover~~ in the original study.

(6) There was no relation between class rank at graduation and a student's looks; there

was also no relation between ~~what~~ a student's starting salary ~~was~~ and ~~how~~ a student^*'s* looked^*s*.

(7) However, after five years on the job, the most attractive graduates earned 9 percent more
on average than ~~were the likely earnings for~~ the least attractive graduates ^*earned* . (8) Fifteen years

later, the most attractive earned 13 percent more.

(9) The question is whether this is the result of law firms' discriminating against
unattractive lawyers, or ^*the result of* clients' preferring attractive lawyers. ~~is the cause of it.~~ (10) Do

unattractive people have a claim to legal protection from discrimination in the workplace?

(11) For example, a cosmetics company could not refuse to hire a salesperson based on his or
her race, but is it the same thing to refuse to hire a salesperson ^*based on his or her* ~~because of the way he or she~~

looks?

◆ 20-1 Using Words Effectively

1. chocolates 2. booming 3. down parka 4. rancid 5. toot on

6. Overweight adolescents ~~who are too heavy~~ may risk serious health problems as adults ~~after they~~ mature.

7. ~~It is a fact that~~ ᵀthe candidates will name their running mates ~~before~~ ^within two weeks ~~have had a chance to~~ pass.

8. I have ~~very often entertained the idea~~ ^believe that a person's ~~garments~~ ^clothes are a ~~manner or~~ means of nonverbal communication.

9. ~~In this day and age~~ ^Today, crime is many people's / ~~top~~, number one concern.

10. When my parents first moved in, their house was ~~originally~~ painted yellow. ~~in color.~~

11. ~~Despite the fact that~~ ^Although they tried not to think about their daughter's death, the ~~horrible~~ tragedy of the accident never fully left them.

12. ~~Practitioners of the medical profession~~ ^Doctors issue the warning that ~~inhaling the smoke of burning tobacco rolled in white paper has the effect of bringing about~~ ^smoking is unhealth~~iness~~. ^y

13. We believe it is time the negotiators ~~laid their cards on the table~~ ^communicated honestly and worked out an end to the strike. _____

14. The counsellor really ~~hit the nail on the head~~ ^diagnosed our difficulty when she said that our problem is lack of trust in each other. _____

15. A person has to be ~~strong as an ox~~ ^Arnold Schwarzenegger to get that little lid off an aspirin bottle. _____

16. When he tinkers with his motorcycle, my brother is <u>intent as Dr. Frankenstein making adjustments to his creation.</u>   C

17. When my former boyfriend broke our date to the prom, it was <u>the ~~straw that broke the~~ ^end of our relationship. ~~camel's back~~.</u> _____

18. Compassion is a trait that separates ~~man~~ ^humans from the animals.

19. ~~Female~~ ^S^ stockbroker Chris Davidson will offer investment strategies at next week's

seminar.

20. Public schools are turning to business~~men~~ ^leaders^ in our community for support in offering job

training.

◆ 20-2 Using Words Effectively

Other correct answers are possible.

(1) I had been attending college in ~~the urban city of~~ Philadelphia for two quarters, / ^or^

~~which is the equivalent of~~ six months. (2) However, getting used to city life was turning out

to be ~~easier said than done~~ ^difficult for me.^

(3) The crowded streets were ~~not very nice~~ ^intimidating^ for someone who grew up in a small town,

and the stench of hot pretzels mixed with automobile fumes and garbage ^C^ was ~~unpleasant~~ ^disgusting.^

(4) Walking to the subway, I ~~stepped around~~ ^skirted^ a pile of rags only to realize ~~and come to the~~

~~conclusion~~ that it was a person ~~lying~~ ^sprawled^ on the ground, asleep.

(5) When I reached Chestnut Street, I heard a voice ~~saying~~ ^crying,^ "Repent! The Lord is angry!

You shall feel His wrath!" (6) It was a man wearing a torn houndstooth jacket, stained ^C^

polyester pants, one penny loafer, and one high-top sneaker. (7) His hair was grayish yellow

~~in color~~ and looked ~~dirty~~ ^greasy.^ (8) He pointed ~~one, single~~ ^a^ finger at me and began to ~~move~~ ^lunge^ in my

direction. (9) Feeling as though I was ~~between a rock and a hard place~~ ^under siege,^ I stepped off the curb

to avoid him, only to hear the ~~sound~~ ^blare^ of a horn and narrowly miss being crushed ^C^ by a bus.

(10) ~~Adding insult to injury,~~ ^To make matters worse,^ the ~~unusual~~ ^crazy^ man said, "Take that as a warning, my friend,

because you might have been killed." ~~Despite the fact that~~ ^Although^ I knew I was not deserving of the

wrath of heaven, I almost believed him. (11) Could this be ~~the straw that broke the camel's~~
~~back~~? ^the incident that sent me over the edge?^

(12) On down the street, I ~~made a transaction for~~ ^bought^ a cheesesteak from a street vendor,

which tasted ~~good~~ ^delicious,^ and I began to feel better. (13) I stopped to listen to a saxophonist playing

a bluesy number, and ~~it was my feeling~~ ^I felt^ at that moment that I had never heard such

~~beautifully spiritual~~ ^C^ music. (14) A ^bone-thin^ woman ~~of an elderly nature~~ in ragged clothes ~~and thin as~~

a rail also stopped, and I ~~took notice of~~ her eyeing my sandwich. (15) Impulsively, ~~and~~
                    d   C

~~without thinking~~, I offered it to her, saying "I can't really eat any more." (16) She smiled and

accepted, and I smiled back. (17) For a moment, ~~in time~~, the three of us were connected ~~in~~

~~that place~~, and the summer night began to seem ~~pretty as a picture~~. (18) For the first time, I
there,   intoxicating.

felt as though the city and I had reached a truce, and I realized ~~in the final analysis~~ that I
                                                                      finally

might learn to like it here.

◆ **21-1 Run-Ons and Comma Splices**

Other correct answers are possible.

1. The soft drink Seven-Up originally got its name from its ingredients~~,~~. It is a blend of
                                                                            I
    seven natural flavors, not just lemon and lime. _____

2. Scientists have a theory about the different sizes of our toes. ~~t~~hey believe the smaller
                                                                    T
    outer toes allow us to balance more effectively. _____

3. A burnt-out lightbulb makes a rattling sound when shaken~~,~~ the filament has broken,
                                                            because
    causing the bulb to fail. _____

4. The command *sic*, which is used to instruct a dog to attack, is a variation of the word

    "seek." __C__

5. Most hot dogs today actually don't have skins~~,~~; however, they may seem to because the

    exterior is firmer than the interior. _____

6. Even plain M & M candies have peanuts in them, ~~they~~ are ground up and mixed in with
                                                    which
    the chocolate. _____

7. The reason the letters *Q* and *Z* are not on a telephone dial is that only twenty-four

    letters were needed and *Q* and *Z* are the least commonly used letters in English. __C__

8. Birds' toes have an amazing locking mechanism allowing them to perch on a branch or

    wire without falling off~~,~~; in fact, birds can stand just as easily on one leg as on two.

    _____

9. No one really knows why we have earlobes/; their only function seems to be to hold earrings. _____

10. Blushing is caused by the dilation of blood vessels and the subsequent flow of more blood to the surface of the body. __C__

11. The white stuff on baseball card gum is powdered sugar, <u>which</u> ~~it~~ is sprinkled on to keep the pieces from sticking together. _____

12. Invented in 1885, Dr Pepper is the oldest major soft-drink brand on the market. __C__

13. Brown chocolate contains cocoa powder, <u>but</u>^ white chocolate does not. _____

14. A greenish potato chip is completely safe to eat. <u>T</u>the green tinge comes from chlorophyll. _____

15. Some people believe that the brand name Kodak was chosen because it sounds like a camera shutter clicking, <u>but</u>^ this is not true. _____

16. There is a good reason we take our temperatures with a thermometer in our mouths or other body cavities/; the idea is to find out the body's internal temperature. _____

17. The hair of a cat is the most electrostatic of any pet hair, <u>which</u> ~~this~~ may be why cat hair is so much worse about sticking to our clothing. _____

18. The skin over our elbows is quite wrinkled, while the skin over our knees is much less so. __C__

19. Only female mosquitos bite/; in fact, male mosquitos do not even have a mouth able to pierce skin. _____

20. Milk gets just as cold in a refrigerator as water; it just doesn't feel as cold in the mouth. _____

◆ **21-2 Run-Ons and Comma Splices**

①It is well known that some female insects and spiders eat the males during and after mating/. <u>T</u>the praying mantis and the black widow spider are two examples. (2) Scientists have always believed that the males were eaten because they weren't able to get away. (3) The

male, it was assumed, would try to survive to breed again, *while* the female simply considered the

male as food. (4) The two were seen as antagonists in a real-life "battle of the sexes."

(5) However, a new discovery seems to cast doubt on this assumption. *It* involves the

poisonous redback spider of Australia. (6) During mating, the male redback actually turns

over and over, maneuvering himself into a position that makes it easier for the female to eat

him. (7) At the same time, the female begins to chew and liquefy the male/; then she

devours him.

(8) The male offers himself up for sacrifice to his mate in order to ensure the

fertilization of the eggs. *This* means that his genes will carry on for another generation.

(9) Competition among male redbacks for females is strong, and a male generally has at most

one chance to mate. (10) For reasons that remain mysterious, a female who doesn't eat her

mate is far less likely to bear his offspring than one who does. (11) The eating ritual does

prolong the act of intercourse, *which* may increase the likelihood of the male's sperm fertilizing

the female's eggs. (12) The male may also provide nutrients that increase the devouring

female's fertility/; therefore, she may lay more eggs.

(13) Female redbacks seem to be superior to males in several ways. *For* one thing, the

male is only about 2 percent the size of the female. (14) The female is brightly colored, while

the male is drab. (15) The male's adult life lasts only a week or so, *but* females live for up to two

years. (16) The male will likely have a chance to mate no more than once/; on the other

hand, the female can have a number of partners over the course of her life.

(17) One study has shown that a devoured male on average fertilizes twice as many eggs

as one who is not eaten. (18) A surviving male even seems to recognize his failure. (19) He

remains in the female's web instead of seeking another mate/; then, he dies within a day or two.

◆ **22-1   Sentence Fragments**

(1) The origin of Valentine's Day is uncertain/, (2) *A*lthough it certainly dates back more

than a thousand years. (3) The holiday honors St. Valentine/, (4) *a* Christian martyr who was supposedly beheaded on February 14 in the year 270. (5) This was the date of an ancient

Roman fertility festival, but the early church replaced it/ (6) ᵂẄith a feast day honoring St.

Valentine. (7) However, the holiday continued to be associated with lovers. (8) By the 1500s,

lovers were exchanging tokens of affection on St. Valentine's Day/, (9) ˢ⫰uch as gloves, garters,

and items decorated with hearts and flowers. (10) The 1700s saw the introduction of the

Valentine card. (11) Originally, these ˡʷᵉʳᵉ handmade of paper lace with a handwritten love poem.

(12) They might even include a satin heart containing a small present.

(13) Within a hundred years, Valentine cards were being produced commercially.

(14) This development ~~leading~~ ˡᵉᵈ to a great expansion of the holiday's popularity. (15) These

Valentine cards were often very elaborate/ (16) Ånd decorated with cupids or flowers.

(17) Some card manufacturers began to produce funny and even insulting Valentines/,

(18) ᵂẄhich continue to be popular today. (19) It is estimated that millions of Valentines are

now exchanged every year in the United States alone. (20) This adds up to a billion-dollar

business/, (21) Íncluding all the candy, flowers, and other gifts that are exchanged, as well.

◆ 22-2 Sentence Fragments

(1) Many experts in the music industry ᵃʳᵉ expecting Tejano to become the United States'

next big music sensation. (2) Tejano is a fusion of Latin pop and country and western music/,

(3) ᵂẄhich is sung with Spanish lyrics. (4) It is a music of the U.S.–Mexican border/,

(5) ʳℛepresenting the culture of Texas's Hispanic community. (6) Tejano's biggest following

now is found in the American Southwest. (7) However, recording executives expect this style

of music eventually to reach a far wider general audience in the United States and Mexico/,

(8) ᵖṔartly because its beat is a little bit raunchy but wholesome at the same time. (9) ᴵᵗ ⁱˢ ᵃẢlready

one of the recording industry's most profitable specialities.

(10) Tejano came to national media attention after the murder of the singer Selena/,

(11) ᵂẄho was on her way to becoming Tejano's first cross-over star. (12) Selena had many

adoring fans. (13) In fact, only six months after her death, at least 619 newborn girls had

been given her name/ (14) Ín Texas alone. (15) The next big star on the horizon is Emilio

Navaira, (16) ~~A~~ ^a singer who is now known simply as Emilio. (17) Emilio has won the male entertainer of the year award at the Tejano Music awards for several years running, (18) ~~And~~ ^a has had several big hits on the Billboard charts. (19) Emilio is popular with Tejano fans for a stage movement called the "Emilio shuffle." (20) He also sings country and western songs in English, (21) ~~Which~~ ^w is unusual for a Tejano musician.

◆ **23-1   Subject-Verb Agreement**

1. honors 2. are 3. visit 4. leave 5. has 6. is 7. appear 8. is
9. finds 10. do 11. teach 12. do 13. are 14. seems 15. see 16. comes
17. casts 18. has 19. eat 20. believe

◆ **23-2   Subject-Verb Agreement**

1. are, C, earn 2. C, are 3. have, C, appear 4. has 5. C, has 6. are 7. is
8. does, has, C 9. C, sing, make, understand 10. find 11. have, C 12. is
13. C, takes, gets 14. C, has 15. are

◆ **24-1   Illogical Shifts**

Other correct answers are possible.

1. ~~A person~~ ^{People} who listens to very loud music may damage their hearing. _____

2. The dark clouds and thunder seemed to be getting closer, so we begin ^a to gather up our towels and beach chairs. _____

3. Hollywood's Dorothy Arzner directed the silent film *Fashions for Women* in 1927, ~~and~~ ^{; she also directed} such sound pictures as *Merrily We Go to Hell* and *Dance Girl Dance.* ~~were also directed by her.~~ _____

4. Anyone over the age of sixty-five should have ~~your~~ ^{his or her} heart checked annually. _____

5. ~~A teacher~~ ^{T s} should not have their own children in any class that they teach. _____

6. The sign warns people using the pool that ~~you~~ ^{they} have to be careful when no lifeguard is present. _____

7. The officer asked, ^{"Can I} ~~could she~~ see ~~my~~ ^{your} driver's license?" _____

8. Last year I worked up to fifty hours a week, but this year I am trying to cut back on my hours. __C__

9. The play was written by Regina Taylor ~~,~~ and she ~~also~~ starred in its original production. *(wrote the play above crossed out "The play was written by"; "and" inserted with caret)*

   _____

10. Police officers must go through rigorous training before receiving ~~his or her~~ *their* badge.

    _____

11. My high school English teacher always said ~~,~~ *that* "you are not supposed to end a

    sentence with preposition." _____ *(Y above "you")*

12. College students who work have to budget ~~your~~ *their* time carefully. _____

13. After the second victim ~~was~~ *is* discovered, the detective in the movie decides to take

    the case. _____

14. A patient who is optimistic about ~~their~~ *his or her* recovery can generally heal more quickly. _____

15. Healthy dieters eat a lot of protein and carbohydrates, but *they avoid* fats and sweets. ~~are avoided

    by them.~~ _____

16. When the emcee asked ~~were~~ *if* they *were* having a good time, the audience members roared

    their approval. _____

17. When a woman is pregnant, ~~you~~ *she* should eat nutritiously. _____

18. The lease states that the occupant cannot put any nails in the walls. __C__

19. As soon as the dishes were done, in walk*ed* ~~s~~ Alvin asking if he could help. _____

20. Even though ~~they~~ *he or she* may not realize it, every child has developed a particular learning

    style by the age of ten. _____

◆ 24-2 Illogical Shifts

Other correct answers are possible.

① For a recent newspaper article, a reporter asked some experts how ~~will~~ people's

eating habits *will* change in the future~~?~~. ② One important change is that ~~a person~~ *people* will be more

likely to work in their home, and the average business day will also expand to match up with

business hours around the world. ③ Consequently, more people will eat takeout meals,

and *they will order* more prepared meals such as pizza. ~~will be ordered by them.~~

(4) One expert says that within ten years people will have diagnostic machines preparing their meals; he predicted~~s~~ that if ~~a person~~ *people* eat~~s~~ too much, these machines will tell ~~you~~ *them* to exercise. (5) Others predict that food will be healthier. (6) Biologists will breed cows to produce lower-fat milk, and *they will develop* leaner pork. ~~will also be developed by them.~~ (7) Fat-free frying may become a reality, allowing ~~a~~ fried food lover*s* to enjoy their favorite treats with none of the pound-inducing fat.

(8) Americans in the future are also likely to consume a more international cuisine. (9) In fact, it is common for people today to eat much spicier food than ~~you~~ *they* ate in years past. (10) One expert actually says that "Americans use sixty-eight more spices than they did just ten years ago."

(11) The most frightening prediction concerns the population explosion. (12) If the Earth's human population doubles in the next forty years as some predict, then producing enough food to feed everyone and provide ~~them with~~ adequate nutrition will be a great challenge.

◆ 25-1 Dangling and Misplaced Modifiers

Other correct answers are possible.

1. Working at my computer, I felt my eyes start to hurt.

2. Looking carefully at the diamond, the dealer found its flaws.

3. Feeling its way around the dark basement, the cat finally discovered the mice.

4. Trying to grab the flying ball, I let it slip out of my hand.

5. Frustrated by their low grades, the students made many complaints.

6. Referring to the instructions, I was able to fill out the form easily.

7. Gathered in the church, the guests waited for the bride to appear.

8. Mixed with water and sugar, cocoa powder makes a tasty beverage.

9. Found on the hospital's doorstep, the baby had been abandoned by its parents.

10. Uplifted by the music, I was overcome with a wonderful feeling.

11. Cheryl passed around cookies on a big tray to everyone.

12. In his new car, my brother drove to meet his girlfriend.

13. *Jurassic Park* is a novel by Michael Crichton about dinosaurs who take over the world.

14. Following its success, the novel was turned into a movie.

15. Rubbing his elbow, Glenn grimaced in pain from his tennis injury.

16. Stretched out in front of the fireplace, the dog seemed to be in seventh heaven.

17. Melissa poured the nuts mixed in with the pretzels into the bowl.

18. With their protests and strikes, the hospital workers are demanding more pay.

19. My sister admired the graceful horse with its flowing mane.

20. Running out of his room in his slippers, Oscar saw the raging fire.

◆ **25-2 Dangling and Misplaced Modifiers**

Other correct answers are possible.

(1) It is no coincidence that Bill Gates, founder of Microsoft, ranks among the wealthiest individuals in the world. (2) ~~He~~ *In the eleventh grade, he* told a friend that he would be a millionaire by the time he was thirty. ~~in the eleventh grade.~~ (3) Having said this, by the age of thirty-one ~~the world saw him~~ *he became* ~~become~~ the youngest self-made billionaire ever. (4) The secret of Gates's success is that, while possessing technical insight, he also saw how computers could be used in people's daily lives. (5) Pondering the issue, ~~it became clear to~~ Gates *saw* how computer software could be marketed as an indispensable tool for the workplace and home. (6) When Microsoft was founded in 1975, most people *going about their daily lives* had never given computers a thought. ~~going about their daily lives.~~ (7) Today, influencing almost every aspect of our lives, ~~many people use~~ computers *are used* both at work and at home. (8) Meanwhile, Gates must be thinking of the six billion people inhabiting the globe ~~in their homes~~ and trying to figure out how he can get them all to use Microsoft products/ *in their homes.* (9) Thinking like a true entrepreneur, ~~the fortune of~~ this man may increase *his fortune* still further.

◆ **26-1 Verbs: Past Tense**

1. departed 2. started 3. selected, lived 4. purchased 5. raised

1. started 2. agreed, earned 3. received, collected 4. applied, accepted
5. discovered, caused 6. believed 7. accused, scored 8. apologized, answered

◆ 26-2   Verbs: Past Tense

1. was, came   2. stood, woke, seemed   3. had, knew   4. appeared, spread
5. took, saw   6. died, could, lost   7. fell, spent   8. became, felt
9. began, shrank, ended   10. were, kept   11. made   12. heard, used   13. chose
14. did, awoke   15. brought, thought   16. spoke, rang   17. broke, kept
18. cost, grew, caught   19. would   20. passed, taught, gave

◆ 27-1   Verbs: Past Participles

1. taken, paid   2. found, stuck, wound   3. hurt, allowed   4. grown, kept
5. held, lost   6. told, improved, said   7. led, made, read, noticed   8. fought, chosen
9. been, written   10. known, eaten, drunk   11. had gained   12. has, held
13. had felt   14. have met   15. had broken, had made   16. had waited, had passed
17. have taken, has been   18. had, seen   19. have told   20. had burned (had burnt)

◆ 27-2   Verbs: Past Participles

1. influenced, has begun   2. C, brought, have chosen   3. have eaten   4. C, filled
5. have been, have caught   6. prejudiced, have led   7. C   8. had risen, has paved
9. had become, used   10. have seen, have turned   11. has taken, has grown, have fallen

◆ 28-1   Nouns and Pronouns

1. I   2. Mothers-in-law   3. her   4. its   5. he or she   6. I   7. he   8. them, us
9. children   10. themselves   11. its   12. it   13. its   14. She   15. species
16. his or her   17. they, its   18. me   19. me   20. her

◆ 28-2   Nouns and Pronouns

(1) Last fall, my friend Paul and ~~me~~ [I] volunteered to help out at the Arts Day Festival on the stree~~tes~~ [streets] of downtown Sarasota. (2) The festival includes ten different performance sites, and each of these sites has ~~their~~ [its] own line-up of different performances throughout the day. (3) ~~It said~~ [According to a notice] in the paper~~,~~ ~~that~~ festival organizers needed people to stage-manage and emcee each site, and ~~us~~ [we] two decided that sounded like fun. (4) We were assigned to a site far from the center of operations, which made Paul and ~~I~~ [me] a little nervous. (5) Our first act was a percussion group, which had to get all ~~their~~ [its] instruments to another site twelve blocks away as soon the second act was to begin. (6) Paul and I~~, we~~ ran around for twenty minutes trying to find some sort of transportation, but finally the musicians had to carry the drums ~~theirselves~~ [themselves], with some help from audience members. (7) Next came a group of circus performers, including children~~s~~ and teenagers in a circus training program, as well as professionals from the Center Stage Circus. (8) The audience gave ~~their~~ [its] biggest applause to a team of acrobats

and to a hilarious dog act. (9) Every time the dog trainer started a new trick, either a brown

poodle or a white terrier would hop down from ~~their~~ ^{its} stand and jump through a hoop, while

the trainer pretended to be upset. (10) The boys and girls in the audience laughed ^{them} ~~theirselves~~

silly over those two little dogs.

(11) Our next act was a one-man band who had recently been one of the runner^s-up~~s~~ in

a national competition. (12) He was interrupted, however, by the arrival of the one-hundred-

member All County Junior High Honor Band. (13) Each of the five band directors took ^{his or her} ~~their~~

turn conducting this group, which seemed to be playing its very best. (14) Then the one-man

band and his singing partner performed their act for the last hour or so.

(15) I don't think any of the other volunteer stage managers had as many different kinds

of acts as Paul and ^I ~~me~~, which made our job a bit challenging. (16) Furthermore, anyone who

manages that site next year should make sure that ^{he or she has} ~~they have~~ plenty of help when it comes

time to take down all the folding chairs!

◆ 29-1 Adjectives and Adverbs

1. good 2. slowly, steadily 3. worse 4. more politely 5. really, badly
6. finest 7. most conservative 8. wildly 9. good, well 10. snugly, tight
11. most intense 12. sooner 13. these, this 14. better 15. quietly
16. sweeter, fully 17. favorably 18. badly, impressive 19. calmly, more furious
20. shortest

◆ 29-2 Adjectives and Adverbs

(1) Among the most difficult~~est~~ environmental problems we face is the effect of gasoline-

burning engines on the Earth's atmosphere. (2) Yet, it is real^{ly} hard to imagine most of the

developed world giving up automobiles. (3) Most drivers feel quite suspicious~~ly~~ about

attempts to limit the use of cars or to force drivers to use public transportation ^{more} often~~er~~.

(4) Consequently, cars are likely to survive, for better or for wors^e~~t~~.

(5) It is likely, however, that cars of the future will become ~~more~~ friendl^{ier}y to the

environment. (6) Even within the next ten years, cars will start to undergo some true^{ly}

fundamental changes. (7) For example, a standard car will have two different fuel sources.

(8) One will be an internal combustion engine that runs very efficient^{ly}, getting up to 70 miles

per gallon burning an oil-based fuel. (9) However, this engine will be used only to accelerate

quick^ly. (10) The system will switch to compressed gas or electricity for cruising speeds,

resulting in less~~er~~ pollution, which will be ~~well~~ good for the environment.

(11) Trains are also expected to become more efficient~~ly~~ and to run ~~more~~ fast^er. (12) In

fact, Amtrak is already in the process of developing the speedi~~er~~st equipment possible, with

trains capable of speeds of more than 150 miles an hour. (13) If trains can eventually run this

~~good~~well, perhaps people will be ^more willing~~er~~ to give up their cars.

◆ **31-1 Using Commas**

1. Born in 1844, Sarah Winnemucca Hopkins was an educator, a lecturer, and a writer.

    _____

2. Her 1883 biography, *Life among the Paiutes,* was one of the earliest published works by a

    Native American woman. _____

3. A member of the Northern Paiute tribe, Winnemucca was born near Humboldt Lake,

    Nevada. _____

4. Her maternal grandfather was leader of the Paiutes living in what later became

    northeastern California, southern Oregon, and western Nevada. _____

5. In her biographical work, Winnemucca Hopkins records the difficulties faced by the

    Paiutes when their lands were taken over by white settlers from the East. _____

6. For example, the Paiutes were skilled in hunting and fishing. _____

7. U.S. government forces, however, confined the tribe to lands that required skill in

    farming. _____

8. Therefore, the tribe almost entirely lost its independence. _____

9. Moreover, the tribe's most valuable lands, part of the Pyramid Lake Reservation, were

    robbed by the railroad lines in 1867. _____

10. A skilled linguist, Winnemucca became a spokesperson for her people in the 1870s.

   _____

11. She visited governmental agencies in Carson City, Nevada, and San Francisco, California, to present her case about the treatment of the Paiutes. _____

12. Her work for her people, unfortunately, had little effect. _____

13. In spite of her efforts, the Paiute tribe was forcibly relocated to a reservation near Yakima, Washington, far from their ancestral lands. _____

14. After marrying a man from Virginia, Winnemucca Hopkins moved with him to Boston.

   _____

15. With the support of several prominent women in the community, she began to lecture throughout the Northeast. _____

16. Her subjects were the unfair treatment of Native American people, the difficulty of life on reservations, and the need for changes in U.S. government policies. _____

17. A highly controversial figure, she was often criticized in the press. _____

18. She felt, nevertheless, that it was necessary to bring public attention to the wrongs suffered by native peoples. _____

19. Late in her life, she started the Peabody School, the first educational institution for Native Americans run by Native Americans. _____

20. She died on October 17, 1891, while visiting her sister, and is buried in Henry Lake, Montana. _____

◆ **31-2 Using Commas**

   (1) The tropical rainforests are home to some of the most amazing creatures in the world. (2) The habitat of the golden toads, for example, is a single square-mile of mountain-top in the rainforest of Costa Rica, the only place on Earth where they are found. (3) In addition, the basilisk lizard is found inside the rainforest. (4) Amazingly enough, this lizard

can actually run on the surface of the water from one side of a pond to the other. (5) Among the most beautiful birds in the world, male quetzals are also dependent on their rainforest habitat. (6) Neither the golden toad, the basilisk, nor the quetzal can survive outside the rainforest. (7) To preserve them, we must work to preserve their habitat.

(8) In addition to such animals, tropical plants in the rainforests provide the main compounds in many drugs. (9) Quinine, for instance, is extracted from the cinchona tree, a native of the rainforest. (10) Quinine is essential for the treatment of malaria, a disease that kills more than a million people in Africa every year. (11) With the destruction of the rainforest, this important cure for malaria might be lost. (12) The rosy periwinkle, another rainforest native, is also endangered; two drugs derived from this plant are used in the fight against cancer. (13) Medicines from other rainforest plants are used to treat ulcer problems, heart problems, and infections. (14) In fact, medical research about cures for many diseases focuses on species from the rainforest. (15) More than 80,000 plants throughout the rainforest have yet to be tested for their effectiveness in cancer treatment, for example. (16) Already endangered, many of these plants may never have a chance to be tested as potential cures.

◆ **32-1 Using Apostrophes**

1. This brochure explains your college's admissions policies. _____

2. Some movie stars' careers′ did not start so brightly. _____

3. One famous actor supported himself for years by selling women's′ shoes. _____

4. The players were concerned because Coach Brown did′n't show up for practice. _____

5. Many parents' child-care problems will be solved by the new center. _____

6. Warmed by the sun's rays, the dog began to wag it′s tail. _____

7. It's odd, I know, but I can never remember that joke's′ punchline. _____

8. We must strive to protect all children's′ rights and to ensure that their′s is a happy future. _____

9. Doctor's have discovered that this tree's bark may hold a cure for cancer. _____

10. The children's clinic is open six days a week. _____

11. The firefighter's' union is threatening a strike. _____

12. Some people think Aretha Franklin's greatest recording is "Respect." _____

13. Is that opinion the same as yours? __C__

14. Students have complained about the smell in the library, but so far their complaints haven't done much good. _____

15. Three workers lost their lives when the factory exploded. __C__

16. Many parents are calling for that principal's resignation. _____

17. A homeless person's greatest enemy is the indifference of other's. _____

18. A single act of kindness can make a big difference in many people's lives. _____

19. Last year, the hockey team had it's best season ever. _____

20. The Kramdens' upstairs neighbors and best friends' are the Nortons. _____

◆ 32-2 Using Apostrophes

(1) When you share a pizza with someone, your friend's way of tasting it may be very different from your's. (2) Tastes vary because people's tongues have different numbers of taste buds. (3) Although scientists have known about genetic taste differences for years, they've only recently discovered that some people actually have many more taste buds' than other people do. (4) These supertasters' tongues have up to one hundred times more taste buds than a nontaster's tongue. (5) When a nontaster eats a particular food, it's taste may be almost nonexistent. (6) Supertasters, however, will taste the same food quite intensely because there's a greater number of taste buds in their mouths to be stimulated. (7) These wide differences in tasting ability account for a food's acceptance or lack of acceptance by different people. (8) In a recent experiment, for example, some children's responses to cheddar

cheese were tested. (9) Most of the supertasters in the group didn't like it. (10) The nontasters, however, liked it very much. (11) Researchers were not surprised by the supertasters' response to the cheese because its̶ ingredients include some elements that are especially bitter to such tasters.

(12) Interestingly, a woman's chance of being a supertaster is much greater than that of a man. (13) In fact, some researcher̶'s' findings show that two-thirds of those identified as supertasters are women. (14) Another discovery is that women tend to find intensely sweet flavors unpleasant, while it's just the opposite for men. (15) Women's̶ dislike for sweet tastes may be genetic, although one researcher thinks it may have more to do with the fear of gaining weight. (16) If researchers are correct, there's probably a genetic link between alcoholism and taste buds, too. (17) Because children who̶'s̶ *se* parents are alcoholics are often nontasters, there seems to be a direct connection between the two. (18) A nontaster's ability to drink considerable alcohol may be due in part to the fact that the nontaster does̶'n't experience alcohol as being so bitter as others do. (19) With an awareness of these different tasters' existence, a food company may do well to reconsider it̶'s marketing strategies.

◆ 33-1 Understanding Mechanics

1. The researcher from Stanford ᵁuniversity said, "ᵀthe experiment is a success." _____

2. As my best ᶠFriend Deanice always says, "ᵂwhat goes around, comes around." _____

3. At the end of the short story "ᵀthe ᴸlottery," Mrs. ᴴhutchinson screams, "ᴵit isn't fair, it isn't right." _____

4. Actress Cicely Tyson won an ᴱemmy for the television movie ᵀthe ᴬautobiography of ᴹmiss ᴶjane ᴾpittman, and she was nominated for an ᴼoscar for the theatrical movie ˢsounder.

   _____

5. An article in the magazine <u>Christopher Street</u> quotes model Christy Turlington as saying, "ᵂwe definitely have great strength being women." _____

6. The class president reminded the graduating seniors of Rosemont high school that they had to return their caps and gowns by friday afternoon. _____

7. When judge Allanson asked whether the witness was prejudiced against latino and asian-american citizens, the defense attorney shouted, "I object"! _____

8. When Rashaad Salaam accepted his heisman trophy, he said that the position coach at colorado state deserved his special thanks. _____

9. The monster in Mary Shelley's novel frankenstein laments, everywhere, I see bliss from which I alone am irrevocably excluded." _____

10. Politicians in washington, d.c., must certainly be glad that in the movie Dirty Harry Clint Eastwood said, go ahead, make my day." _____

11. The Guinness book of world records notes that the largest inhabited castle in the world is Windsor castle at Windsor in great britain. _____

12. In 1648, king charles II granted a three-year charter to the first union in the United states, which was named the shoemakers and booters union. _____

13. Gwendolyn Brooks's poem a Song in the front yard" begins with the line "I've stayed in the front yard all my life." _____

14. Singer sonja marie performed the song and i gave my love to you" on the soundtrack of the movie waiting to exhale. _____

15. "In spite of everything," wrote Anne Frank, "I still believe that people are really good at heart." _____

16. In his book "Do Penguins have knees?," David Feldman asks, why is our mathematical vocabulary a seemingly random hodgepodge of greek and latin terminology?" _____

17. The statue of Liberty stands on ellis island in the harbor of New York city. _____

18. A doctor must earn a medical degree and pass state boards before being allowed to set up a practice, according to the publication _Know Your Rights as a Patient._ __C__

19. "Remove paper before loading," warns the label on my new *H*ewlett *P*ackard brand

   printer. _____

20. The *W*ashington *P*ost recently broke a story about plots to bomb the offices of the
   *F*ederal *A*viation *C*ommission and the *W*orld *W*atch *O*rganization. _____

◆ 33-2 Understanding Mechanics

   (1) Singer and *A*ctress Ethel *W*aters was the first *A*frican-*A*merican woman to become an
entertainment star in the United *S*tates. (2) She was born to a poor *F*amily in Chester,
*P*ennsylvania, in 1896. (3) As a young woman, she worked as a chambermaid before
achieving the beginnings of success in *S*how *B*usiness at seventeen, performing under the
name *S*weet *M*ama *S*tringbean. (4) An accomplished blues singer, she had hits with such
popular songs as "Dinah" and "*S*tormy *W*eather," and she was particularly associated with the
hymn "His *E*ye *I*s on the *S*parrow."

   (5) On *B*roadway, she starred in a number of popular musicals, including "As *T*housands
*C*heer" and "*C*abin in the *S*ky." (6) She also appeared in the *M*etro *G*oldwyn *M*ayer film version
of "*C*abin in the *S*ky," about which the magazine Variety wrote, "*W*hatever its box office fate, it
is a worthwhile picture for Metro to have made, if only as a step toward *H*ollywood
recognition of the place of the black man in American *L*ife." (7) Waters's greatest *T*riumph
was as the character Berenice *S*adie Brown in the play Member of the Wedding, a role she
repeated in the film version. (8) Set in a small *G*eorgia town, it is the story of a lonely twelve-
year-old girl and the compassionate housekeeper who looks after her. (9) Among her other
films is "*P*inky," for which she received an Academy *A*ward nomination. (10) She also
published two volumes of autobiography, including the best-selling To *M*e *I*t's *W*onderful.

   (11) An active member of the *N*ational *A*ssociation for the *A*dvancement of *C*olored
*P*eople, Waters was instrumental in opening the way for black performers who followed her.

◆ 34-1 Understanding Spelling

1. ninth, annoyed, C   2. supposed, quite   3. hear, C, it's   4. hoping, C, than
5. we're, deceived, daily   6. admitted, C, overreaction   7. C, too, break   8. lose, find
9. Neither, C, definitely   10. Whether, business, judgment   11. C, trapped

12. professor, C, dependent   13. noticeable, C, displayed
14. truly, surprised, C, misspellings   15. C, passed, through   16. you're
17. beliefs, intelligent, arguments   18. C, too, develop
19. appealing, C, responsibility   20. C, effects, separate

◆ **34-2   Understanding Spelling**

(1) Most all of us reco~g~nize that we can perceive ~alot~ *a lot* about people by reading the expressions on their faces. (2) However, it is also poss~a~*i*ble to understand people by refer~r~ing to the~re~ *ir* body language.

(3) For example, it will often be pla~n~*in*e when a person is telling a lie because he or she will fidget a bit. (4) The most common gesture indicat~e~ing a lie is touching the head in some way. (5) Rubbing the back of the neck usu~a~lly suggests that one is tru~e~ly uncertain of what one is saying. (6) Rubbing one's eye or nose can be an unconscien~ce~ *ous* way of covering the dec~ie~*ei*ving words com~m~ing out of one's mouth. (7) This does not mean that you should always disbelieve someone ~who's~ ~every day~ *whose everyday* gestures sometimes include touching the face.
(8) However, when you are uncertain ~weather~ *whether* to trust someone's words, you may want to w~ie~*ei*gh the importance of ~they're~ *their* gestures.

(9) Observ~e~ing how people sit, stand, and move on social occas~s~ions can also be informative. (10) People who stand with their arms and legs crossed are ~generly~ *generally* feeling som~e~what defensive or closed. (11) A hand on the hip suggests confidence, while scratching one's arm or leg may indicate insecur~e~ity. (12) A person who ~sets~ *sits* as part of a group with his or her arms crossed and legs pointed away from the others is lik~e~ly to be feeling withdrawn from the conversation, or at least with~h~olding judgment. (13) One who reclines a bit with his or her hands behind the head is ~probly~ ~quit~ *probably quite* confident and perhaps even feeling superior to the rest of the group. (14) Two people who are close fr~ie~nds and very use~d~ to each other's company will often position themselves on a couch so that they are turned slightly but notic~e~ably toward each other. (15) They may even adopt a very sim~i~lar posture.

(16) While judg~e~ing people by their body language has obvious limitations, it can also be of ben~e~fit as a way of get~t~ing to ~no~ *know* other people.